Cases for Reflection and Analysis

for

Exceptional Learners

Introduction to Special Education

TENTH EDITION

Daniel P. Hallahan

University of Virginia

James M. Kauffman

University of Virginia

PEARSON

Boston   New York   San Francisco   Mexico City   Montreal
Toronto   London   Madrid   Munich   Paris   Hong Kong
Singapore   Tokyo   Cape Town   Sydney

Table of Contents

Preface

The cases we have selected for inclusion in this booklet reflect both the joy and the pain of teachers working with exceptional children. What professors of education and commentators in the popular press write about teaching is often wondrously abstract, hypothetical, or idealistic, and does not ring true for those who work daily in classrooms. In contrast, the stories we call cases are neither abstract descriptions nor conjecture, nor do they reflect an idealism detached from the realities of the classroom. They are true stories of teachers—what really happened as told from the perspectives of real teachers and how they thought and felt about what was happening.

Updates to the Tenth Edition

For the Tenth Edition, we've added four new cases addressing Attention Deficit Hyperactivity Disorder, Communication Disorders, Autism Spectrum Disorders, and Physical Disabilities. In addition to their focus on the categories of disability, you'll find that all of the cases also address the entire range of overarching topics and issues related to special education, including legislation, placement and personnel, collaboration, parents and families, cultural diversity, and others. You'll also notice that we've added to the Tenth Edition of the main text specific references (*Casebook Reflections*) linking text content to relevant aspects of each case. (See the *Quick Guide to the Main Text*, pages xi–xii of this booklet.)

Because of the sensitive nature of much of the information contained in most of the cases, the identities of the teachers who wrote them, as well as the other individuals who are described in their stories, must in most cases be masked. We are grateful to Susan Washko and to the other teachers identified by pseudonyms who told us or wrote the stories comprising these cases. Their willingness to share their experiences has given many other educators priceless opportunities to reflect on the art and science of teaching exceptional children. We are also grateful to our colleagues Robert F. McNergney, Jean Crockett, Anne Sande, and Stephen Byrd for their assistance in obtaining several of the cases.

D. P. H.

J. M. K.

Charlottesville, Virginia

Introduction

This supplement is a collection of cases to use with our text, *Exceptional Learners: Introduction to Special Education*, Tenth Edition (Hallahan & Kauffman, 2006). Some cases were written following interviews with teachers, others were written by teachers or intern teachers. All the cases are factual—they are not hypothetical, and the only changes in the facts of the cases are those necessary to protect the identities of the individuals about whom they are written.

Background

The use of cases in teaching has a long, celebrated history in law and business. Some schools, for example the Harvard Business School and the Darden School of Business at the University of Virginia, use cases as their primary method of instruction. Students analyze and discuss real-life situations that have occurred in the world of business or law. It may be that they address issues surrounding the merger of two Fortune 500 companies, or perhaps they consider the ramifications of an American manufacturing business attempting to open up a market in a foreign country. Whatever the focus of the case, the idea is to get students to consider issues that they are likely to face when they finish their academic work and enter the real world of business.

There is a small, but rapidly growing, number of teacher educators who have started to use cases with preservice teachers, with the idea of enabling teachers to grapple with issues before they enter the real world of teaching in public schools. We are among this group who have been experimenting with case teaching (see Goor & Santos, 2002; Kauffman, 2005; Kauffman, Mostert, Trent, & Pullen, 2006). We are not claiming that all courses in teacher education lend themselves equally to the use of cases, nor do we believe that the case method is every instructor's cup of tea. There is still the need for more traditional formats, such as lectures. In the introduction to special education course, in particular, cases probably cannot provide all of the information that needs to be conveyed. There is reason to believe, however, that cases can serve as a valuable supplement to other forms of classroom instruction.

Rationale

A basic rationale for using cases in teacher education is that it is a way to teach novices to think more like those with more experience and expertise. The case method may be a way of speeding up the socialization process. For several years, James Boyd White, a law professor, has delivered a speech to entering law school students that emphasizes the use of cases in training the "legal mind." Much of what he says holds true for the education profession. One could substitute the word "teacher" for "lawyer" and "education" for "law" in the following quote and depict our view of the value of using cases in teacher education:

> Let me suggest that you regard the law, not as a set of rules to be memorized, but as an activity, as something that people do with their minds and with each other as they act in relation both to a body of authoritative legal material and to the circumstances and events of the actual world. The law is a set of social and intellectual practices that defines a universe or culture in which you will learn to function . . . Our primary aim is not to transmit information to you but to help you learn how to do what it is that lawyers do with the problems that come to them . . .
>
> Of course the law as an activity can and should be studied . . . from the point of view of other disciplines . . . But in studying the law in such ways one is functioning, not as a lawyer, but as an anthropologist, as a historian, and so forth. What is peculiar and central to your experience both in law school and beyond is that you learn how to participate in this activity, not as an academic, but as a legal mind . . .
>
> A[n] analogy [to learning law] may be learning a language. One must of course learn the rules of grammar and the meaning of terms, but to know those things is not to know how to speak the language. That knowledge comes only with use. (White, 1985, pp. 52–53)

Researchers in the area of cognitive science also provide us with grounds to believe that cases can be useful in teacher education. Their research informs us that people learning a complex task (and what could be more complicated than teaching!) learn it best when they can do it under the tutelage of experts whom they can imitate. In an introductory course to special education, it would not be practical, nor would it be ethical, to have students be responsible for solving real problems presented by students with disabilities. The next best thing, however, is to have students consider cases of teaching situations involving students with disabilities. Discussing cases that require solutions to real problems encountered by real teachers, although a step removed from actually having to solve the problems in the natural setting, should be more helpful in making teachers better problem solvers than teachers trained through traditional lecture and discussion formats. Cases provide a narrative of teachers in action. Discussing cases provides a forum for preservice teachers to try out ideas and potential solutions before actually being faced with making those decisions under fire in the classroom. For the inservice teacher, discussing cases provides the opportunity to hone their decision making skills. In this way, then, a case method can serve as a bridge between academia and the classroom.

The Cases

The cases we have chosen for this supplement involve teachers working with students exemplifying a wide range of ages and disabilities, as well as a case involving students who are gifted. Recognizing that many students who will use this supplement are in general education and that more and more students are spending more and more time in regular classes, the focus of most of the cases is on a teaching situation involving a general education setting. We have provided "Questions for Reflection" with each case that are aimed to help you think about some of the major issues of the case. Whenever possible, we have noted links between these questions and specific chapters in the Hallahan and Kauffman text. A complete correlation between the cases in this booklet and the text is shown in the *Quick Guide to the Main Text*, pages xi–xii of this booklet. Also see the *Casebook Reflections* features in the text, which provide additional opportunities to connect and apply the cases to specific text content.

Cautions

We caution that not all of the cases portray best practices or a high level of teacher reflection. It is our experience that it is a rare case that does not contain at least some actions or attitudes of the teacher or teachers that are open to criticism. At the same time, it is a rare case that is totally devoid of good teaching practices. Remember, these are *real* cases, that is, "slices of teaching life." They show teachers in action, in emotionally charged situations that often demand split-second decisions. In fact, by giving you the luxury of time to reflect on such cases, we hope we will be helping you become better decision makers when faced with similar circumstances. Finally, we caution you that our "Questions for Reflection" do not necessarily have one right answer. Moreover, answers are not always found in the Hallahan and Kauffman text—or any other book, for that matter. Teaching is not an endeavor for which there is always a textbook description. Like other professions, teaching demands integrating knowledge from a variety of sources to address problems through intellectually rigorous inquiry and ethically defensible action.

References

Goor, M. B. & Santos, K. E. (2002). *To think like a teacher: Cases for special education interns and novice teachers.* Boston: Allyn & Bacon.

Hallahan, D. P., & Kauffman, J. M. (2006). *Exceptional learners: Introduction to special education.* (10th ed.). Boston: Allyn & Bacon.

Kauffman, J. M. (2005). *Cases in emotional and behavioral disorders of children and youth.* Upper Saddle River, NJ: Prentice Hall.

Kauffman, J. M., Mostert, M. P., Trent, S. C., & Pullen, P. L. (2006). *Managing classroom behavior: A reflective case-based approach* (4th ed.). Boston: Allyn & Bacon.

White, B. (1985). *Heracles' bow: Essays on the rhetoric and poetics of the law.* Madison, WI: University of Wisconsin Press.

The table below lists the main topics addressed by the cases in this booklet alongside the chapters where they are covered in *Exceptional Learners: Introduction to Special Education*, Tenth Edition (Hallahan & Kauffman). Keep in mind that the individuals profiled in these cases reflect the complexities involved in special education issues and the reality that students may have more than one category of special need. Each case touches on special education topics relevant to all categories including cultural diversity, collaboration, transition, parents and families, as well as legal issues, policies, and personnel. Remember to look for the *Casebook Reflection* boxes in the main text and read over the cases that apply to the textbook discussions to enhance your understanding.

CASES	KEY ISSUES	COVERAGE IN *Exceptional Learners: Introduction to Special Education*, Tenth Edition (Hallahan & Kauffman)
Should I Take Juanita Pope?	• Individuals with Disabilities Education Act (IDEA) • Collaboration • Multicultural Issues • Mental Retardation • Learning Disabilities	Chapters 1, 2, 3, 5, & 6
What Do We Do with Jim?	• Multicultural Issues • Parents & Families • Mental Retardation • Emotional or Behavioral Disorders	Chapters 3, 4, 5, & 8
How Did We Miss Jack All These Years?	• Parents & Families • Learning Disabilities • ADHD • Emotional or Behavioral Disorders	Chapters 6, 7, & 8
More Than LD	• Learning Disabilities • ADHD	Chapters 6 & 7

The Red Belt	• Emotional or Behavioral Disorders • Communication Disorders	Chapters 8 & 9
Albert Says What?	• Parents & Families • Communication Disorders	Chapters 3 & 9
Least Restrictive for Whom?	• Parents & Families • Deafness and Hearing Loss	Chapters 4 & 10
The Reluctant Collaborator	• Collaboration • Parents & Families • Blindness and Low Vision	Chapters 2, 4, & 11
Getting to Know Chase	• Autism Spectrum Disorders	Chapter 12
Who Will Help Patrick	• IDEA • Collaboration • Multicultural Issues • Parents & Families • ADHD • Emotional or Behavioral Disorders • Multiple and Severe Disabilities	Chapters 1, 2, 3, 4, 7, 8, & 13
Praying for a Miracle	• Multicultural Issues • Physical Disabilities	Chapters 3 & 14
Filling Mr. K's Shoes— Not!	• Special Gifts and Talents	Chapter 15
Never Give Up	• MR • Learning Disabilities • ADHD • Emotional or Behavioral Disorders • Special Gifts and Talents	Chapters 5, 6, 7, 8, & 15

Should I Take Juanita Pope?

Isabelle Dworkin

During the beginning weeks of school, several sixth grade teachers who worked as a team came to me with a complaint.

"We have a little girl on our unit who definitely belongs in your class."

Later, the principal came to me.

"We may have another little girl for you."

Then the head of the child study team came by.

"Don't get too settled with your numbers [of students], because we may be adding one to your class roll. She's already been referred for child study, and I'll let you know when we have her child study meeting."

Well, with all of these people insinuating that a new body would eventually be placed in my classroom, it was definitely time to find out exactly who Juanita Pope was.

During her early school years, Juanita lived with her mother, Mrs. Pope. She never attended preschool. Mrs. Pope claimed that she was not aware that Juanita could come to school when she was six years old. Therefore, Juanita was not sent to kindergarten until she was 6 years, 9 months old. This confused start in school reflects the state of Juanita's educational history.

Her kindergarten teacher felt that Juanita's strengths were in the areas of fine motor development, self-help, and eagerness to try new things. She was weak in the areas of math and language skills. At the time of her initial evaluation, her adaptive behavior scale scores reflected adequately developed socialization, self-help, and receptive language skills. Juanita was weak in expressive and written language skills. The teacher stated that the scores were influenced by "lack of opportunity in the home environment." The eligibility committee decided she was developmentally delayed—25% delayed in communication, daily living skills, and cognition. IQ: 68. Mental retardation was not suspected due to the "inconsistency of the scores." She was placed in a special "multicategorical" class with some mainstreaming.

1

However, during the next school year, Juanita was beyond the age limit for the multicategorical class, so another child study meeting was held to assess her progress and find another placement. The regular classroom teacher who had her indicated that Juanita was shy and did not ask for help, did well with the "concrete and connecting levels" in math, did not do well with concepts that required making inferences, was successful in a "carefully controlled time period with extra attention," and was not functioning well in the mainstream because her primary deficit was in reading. Eligibility for special education was continued, and she was placed in a self-contained class for students with learning disabilities. IQ: 85.

Juanita was re-evaluated three years later. The fifth-grade mainstream teacher observed that mainstreaming had gone really well. Juanita had made progress in working on her own, interpreting what she read, and asking questions about the teacher's expectations. She was still shy and hesitant to form new relationships, relied on familiar friendships, and needed a great deal of structure and repetition. Juanita's special education teacher taught her math and commented that "Juanita is not a risk-taker." She went on to describe Juanita as interacting in socially appropriate ways with others but having trouble sharing and contributing to a small peer group, having difficulty with problem-solving and higher level thinking, needing extra time to formulate responses, and having trouble with newly introduced concepts. The psychologist found her strongest skills to be in rote numerical reasoning and rote auditory memory. Her weaknesses were in the areas of visual-motor and spatial orientation. IQ: 71. The psychologist's recommendation: "Work must be at her ability level and should probably be presented in small doses." He went on to recommend using concrete instructional materials, giving Juanita rationales for learning new information, and providing assertiveness training to improve her personal and academic skills. The evaluating committee determined that Juanita was ineligible for any special services because her aptitude and achievement scores indicated significant improvement.

Juanita had an academic history of being shifted from program to program. She had been shifted around a lot in her personal life, too. Mrs. Britt, her grandmother, was constantly called by the school when Juanita lived with her mother. Mrs. Pope did not respond to or comply with the school's notes or calls. When Mrs. Pope's marriage to Juanita's father ended, the oldest daughter, Sheila (Juanita's half-sister), was "given" to her father's relatives in a nearby town. Before Mrs. Pope left town, Juanita and her older brother were "given" to Mrs. Britt. (Mrs. Britt's home seemed to be the place where all of Juanita's siblings were taken when Mrs. Pope either changed boyfriends or became pregnant again.) Mrs. Pope could not be found for several years; when she was found, she had given birth to another child. By this time, Juanita had already started relying heavily on adults at school for support.

After discovering all of this information about Juanita's dysfunctional family history and ever-changing classroom settings, I was convinced that someone had to stop this chaos. If the sixth grade team had their way, Juanita was about to go through yet another eligibility merry-go-round. We had not reached the halfway point of the first nine weeks, and the sixth grade teachers were already pleading fervently to have Juanita referred to the child study committee. The sixth grade team had solicited my input, so I felt comfortable asking these teachers this question, which had been going through my mind: "How in the world did they know this child's abilities if she had only been in school for such a short time?"

The sixth grade teachers assured me that they had had a very frustrating time trying to instruct Juanita.

"If you'd read her file, you'd understand why we're doing this so early."

I told them that I'd read Juanita's file, but they needed to consider that she had been placed directly into all her regular classes without any type of transition. Regardless of my comment, they continued to push to have a child study meeting. But the meeting did not come about. Because Juanita had been found ineligible for special education services only at the end of the previous school year, the special education coordinator wanted the team to give Juanita some time to make the transition to regular classes. Needless to say, perhaps, they were extremely disappointed in how the "transition" turned out.

The sixth grade teachers who were supposed to be helping Juanita make the transition started visiting me regularly to ask my opinion or complain about any problems they were having with Juanita. Many of these teachers and their students had always acted as if I had a scarlet "R" on my door (for Retarded Classroom); this was indeed a novelty. Most of the time, regular education teachers never asked my opinion about anything academic. Just because I taught retarded students, did that make me retarded, too?

The teachers' complaints were usually about Juanita's poor comprehension and basic skills, her inability to spell, and her disinterest or inability to respond to the challenges of their classrooms. They often reminded me that they had many more kids than I did, so I might not understand the magnitude of the problem. I commiserated with them, but continued patiently to remind them that this was a transitional year for Juanita and that her work needed to be monitored and adjusted according to her abilities. Inevitably, I either looked at their assignments and suggested ways to modify them or went directly to my shelves or file cabinet to substitute high interest-low vocabulary work for the higher level materials they were constantly giving her. Sometimes the teachers resisted modifying the materials because they thought the modifications would take away from the quality of the project.

Several teachers also complained about Juanita's poor coping skills. Her shyness had always been a controlling factor in her academic and social development. They complained that she was usually nonresponsive during guided practice time. If they waited quietly after asking a question, she would eventually respond. However, waiting for the response sometimes slowed down the pace of the class so severely that the other students started getting off task. If they attempted to stimulate an answer, Juanita became nonresponsive. If they gave her constructive criticism, suggestions, or reprimands, Juanita also "shut down" and cried soundlessly. While in this mode, she refused to give any eye contact whatsoever. The teachers said that they attempted to ignore the "shut downs" but reacted to the crying by allowing her to go to the bathroom to dry her tears and get composed. This was not working, because Juanita would then take two periods to come back; she not only failed to complete the assignment but missed hearing other assignments as well. I suggested that they were giving Juanita this message: "Crying gets you time off task and attention from others." To this suggestion they responded, "But I don't have time to deal with it."

Furthermore, Juanita was conveniently leaving her homework at home, bringing it in incomplete or not done at all (her excuse: "My grandmother doesn't know how to do this," or "I had to help take care of my little brother, so I didn't have time to do it"), not writing down assignments, losing study guides for tests, not studying for tests, misplacing books, and missing days of school.

At the beginning of the school year, I had decided to do free tutoring for students who were on free or reduced-price lunches. I told the guidance counselors to assign two to four children to me, and I would tutor them as long as they needed my help. The end of the first nine weeks had come and gone, and no students had been referred to me. The sixth grade team had already told me that Juanita was struggling to keep up with her classmates. So I approached Mrs. Walker, the sixth grade guidance counselor, about getting Mrs. Britt's permission to tutor Juanita. It seemed like the most logical thing to do. The guidance counselor agreed that it was a good idea. Mrs. Britt gave her permission, but was concerned that Juanita would not agree to the decision. Mrs. Walker and I arranged to have Juanita sent to her office to ask Juanita's permission to include her in the tutoring sessions.

Our priority in the meeting was that Juanita feel comfortable staying after school and riding home with me. I had already attempted to establish a relationship with Juanita by talking to her in the hallways and at lunchtime. Many times, Juanita did not acknowledge my presence. She was very cautious about talking in my presence, but I was persistent because Juanita looked so unhappy going down the hallways. This meeting would be an indicator of whether I had earned her trust.

When she came into the office, Juanita looked at me suspiciously. I decided to take my cue from Mrs. Walker. She showed Juanita her grades on the computer and explained that she was doing okay in her exploratory class and math (she had made a C), but was making D's and F's in all of her other classes. Mrs. Walker explained that I had a way of helping her improve her grades. Having been given my cue, I told Juanita about my proposed tutoring session and asked her if she wanted to participate. She said very quietly, "I have to ask my grandmother." Mrs. Walker then chimed in, "Why don't we call her now?" (Neither of us wanted to alienate Juanita by telling her we had already contacted Mrs. Britt.) Juanita listened while Mrs. Walker and I talked to her grandmother. I explained that the tutoring sessions would probably be two or three times a week, 3:30 to 5:00, never on Fridays; some days we might have to make special arrangements if I had a class or meeting, and I would give Juanita a ride home after every session. Juanita talked to her grandmother on the phone, and when she hung up she agreed to comply with Mrs. Britt's wishes.

"But," I emphasized to her, "this is your decision, too. If you make the decision, you'll more than likely stick with it." She nodded her assent, and we decided to start the tutoring that next day!

Juanita's teachers were happy with this arrangement and agreed to give me copies of future study guides, assignments, and the teacher's manual for the textbooks if necessary.

First tutoring session; no Juanita. After a long search, I finally found her dragging her feet down a distant hallway. I encouraged her to speed up, and when she would not I reminded her that the later she came to the tutoring session the longer we would have to stay to make up the lost time. She immediately quickened her pace, but the minute she came into the room she had to get a drink of water and go to the bathroom. I agreed to let her go to the bathroom after we established the rules for the tutoring session. I also clarified that the tutoring sessions started exactly at 3:30, so from 3:15 to 3:30 she should get her drink of water and go to the bathroom. Once inside the classroom, I would have a snack for her. If she came late to the session, we would stay longer to make up the missed time. She mumbled her "Okay" and began taking unorganized materials from her notebook.

The biggest challenge during our subsequent tutoring sessions was getting Juanita to bring in necessary materials to complete her assignments. I met her "I have no homework" with, "Well, practice makes perfect. Let's go over the assignment from the other day."

Usually, a bad day in class was followed by a horrible tutoring session. The first time Juanita did her crying routine with me it was because she wanted me to give her the answers for her assignment. When I told her that her work was being graded, not mine, the tears began. I continued explaining the assignment to her—ignoring the tears—and she interrupted by saying, "My other teachers let me go get water and go to the bathroom when I get upset." My response: "Well, that's inappropriate behavior. You can't solve any problem by crying and drinking water. We have work to do. I have tissues in my classroom, and if you're thirsty, I'll fill a cup with water while you do your assignment."

Well, the quiet tears were replaced with loud wailing and Juanita's demand that she be allowed to leave the room to wipe her face and nose. After I ignored her demands, Juanita tried her "shut-down" routine, and I told her that I was willing to out wait her. She informed me that she was not going to do any more work, and I replied, "Take your time, because your time is my time." After a long pause, she said she wanted to call her grandmother. "The office is locked up now, and so are the telephones," I reminded her. She then "shut down" again, so I simply "shut down" too. I started grading papers and cleaning up my room, and after 20 minutes of silence, she got up and wiped her nose. "What else do I have to do?"

I would love to say that we always ended our sessions on a positive note, but we didn't. Several times she conveniently forgot our session and went home on the bus or refused to continue studying for tests at home. Also, having used "inventive" spellings for most of her elementary school career, she was having a hard time correcting the spelling in her written work, even when she could use a spellchecker. She continued to lose many points on her papers due to misspelled words. I was very frustrated when some of her graded projects were returned to her. I believed that her sixth grade teachers did not consider her "transitional" status when they graded her assignments. When I approached them about this, they asked, "What would the other kids think if they saw Juanita's grade and the poor quality of her assignment?" No amount of explaining how hard she had worked could get them to change the grade. The language arts teacher came by my classroom to report that Juanita had not completed her daily journal pertaining to a book she was reading silently. I tried to explain that there were limitations to my involvement in Juanita's participation. It seemed to me that they had stopped holding her accountable. They were not expressing their expectations to Juanita. I was supposed to take care of that, too!

Several times Juanita commented, "Why should I stay after school with you if I'm still getting C's and D's?" She had a very valid point, I thought, but I could only encourage her to continue coming to our sessions. Without my intervention, those C's and D's would become F's.

Juanita had failed science in two consecutive semesters. Mrs. Walker came to my classroom and asked to place Juanita in my class for science. The science teacher felt that there was no way that Juanita would ever grasp the subject matter. So, the team suggested either placing her in another study hall or my classroom (because I already had a trusting relationship with Juanita). I told the guidance counselor that this was just another excuse for the regular education teachers not to do their job; but, yes, I would take Juanita for science. At least she would be actively involved in a structured learning environment, not just reading another library book.

Looking somewhat relieved, Juanita came into my classroom. Her skills were quite comparable to my students with mild mental retardation. In the beginning, she did not like being separated from her friends and would not participate. But when I made her the leader of a cooperative learning group, she became more involved, answered questions, and made friends.

We continued the tutoring sessions, and she ended the school year barely passing to the seventh grade. She had managed to get through the school year without another child study meeting being called, but I knew that we would have that to deal with the next school year. True to form, the sixth grade teachers had already warned the seventh grade teams about Juanita Pope.

Three weeks of the first nine were allowed to pass before the child study referral was made. Within these three weeks, the seventh grade teachers had come to some definite conclusions. They had already lowered their expectations and placed her in collaborative classes, but she still had very poor basic skills in all areas, and could not comprehend directions and concepts. Juanita had poor organizational skills, poor peer interactions, a delayed response time, and poor academic and social coping skills. One teacher wrote that she was afraid that Juanita would become "a classic example of a student falling through the cracks" at our school if special services were not reinstated. Juanita was placed in an extra "core" class as an alternative to an "exploratory," a common practice in our school when a student has difficulty in most academic classes. The teacher of the extra core classes did not believe that Juanita was making significant progress because most of her work was of poor quality. Juanita was, as she put it, "spending her time in classes with material that is essentially meaningless to her."

The child study team met and decided to recommend a referral for a special education re-evaluation, have a complete neurological to determine the origin of Juanita's delayed responses, and reduce her academic classes by one.

After the child study team's meeting, I received a visit from the leader of the team. They were searching for some place to put Juanita for that one class. There was no way to reschedule her classes with the other seventh grade team, so they thought of my classroom. Once again, my established, "trusting relationship" was lauded by the regular education teachers. In addition, Juanita was complaining to the seventh grade guidance counselor about having all Caucasian teachers, and they felt that I could provide the African-American influence that Juanita desired. Would I please help them solve this problem?

Were they just feeding my ego, or was it a genuine belief that I could make a difference? Would I once again "save the day" for these regular education teachers, who considered my opinion only when it was time to remove bodies from their classes? Shouldn't these teachers be held accountable for nurturing Juanita's academic development? Couldn't they utilize some of the energy being used to get Juanita out of their classroom to modify her classroom assignments? Or, should I just put these personal feelings aside and put Juanita first?

Questions for Reflection

In what ways does Juanita fit the definition of children "at risk"? Do you think she had a disability (or disabilities)? (Hallahan & Kauffman, Chapter 1)

To what extent do you see evidence that the requirements of IDEA were being met by Juanita's school system? (Hallahan & Kauffman, Chapter 1)

Who do you think should have been responsible for teaching Juanita? To what extent were general and special educators collaborating? What do you see as the central issues in role definitions and expectations of the regular classroom teachers and Isabelle? (Hallahan & Kauffman, Chapters 1 and 2)

Ideally, special and general educators work together to include the student with mild mental retardation (retardation not requiring intensive support services) as much as possible in regular classes. What might Isabelle have done to try to work out such a collaborative arrangement to help Juanita make a successful transition into regular classes? What special problems might she have encountered (Hallahan & Kauffman, Chapters 1, 2, and 5)?

What aspects of this case involve multicultural issues? (Hallahan & Kauffman, Chapter 3)

Whose attitudes and behavior do you find most troubling in this case—Juanita's, the regular classroom teachers', or Isabelle's? Why?

What Do We Do with Jim?

Frieda Bailey

It's been at least 10 years since I have had to deal with a case as difficult as Jim. And, believe me, that's saying a lot. Maybe the fact that I've been in the same school system for so long has something to do with it, but I have had some success with some of the most difficult kids to come through Johnson Middle School. With Jim, though, this is a whole new ballgame.

I didn't go into this profession for the recognition or to brag, but some do say that my classroom is a "well-oiled machine." I try to follow all of the best-practice suggestions that I learned through my graduate program in special education. My students learn (some a little later than others, but most come around to it at their own pace) that there are fundamental rules and guidelines for behavior that we all have to follow to make this class what it is—a place where students eligible for MiMH (Mild Mental Handicaps, perhaps known as EMR or by some other designation in other systems) can be safe and learn. Sure, I individualize for learning and behavior, but there really is a sense of community within this individualization: I've even been asked to give a talk at the local university about how this works in my class.

So, maybe this is one reason (along with having been in the system so long that I sometimes end up teaching the children of my former students!) that other teachers in the school use my classroom as an intermediate step in their time-out discipline procedures. Often, a student will come to my class with a pass from his or her teacher, asking if they can sit in my room for a while to "cooldown." Although I know some of these kids from former years or through their families, when they come to my room with such a pass it's all business. They can come at other times to chat, maybe as a reward for good behavior, but as a time-out I make sure that this is not rewarding or reinforcing for them, for otherwise I'd have the whole school in here, and it would certainly not help the other teachers with their behavior management!

Enter: Jim. This was one of the few times that a teacher sent me a student whom I had not met but was already notorious in the school. OK, I thought, I can handle this. But no matter how much you know or how good you think your system is, there are always a few who fall through the sieve. That day, there must have been particularly large holes in the sieve, because I was not sure I could get this kid to calm down! He came strutting in, slammed the door, and then walked on tiptoes—as slowly as possible—to my desk to hand me the pass, smirking the entire time. I was in the middle of a math lesson, which in my class means that Adam and Jane are using manipulatives to learn how to count by tens, some others are adding to 3 digits, and some are multiplying to 2 digits: it's a dangerous myth that MiMH classes have less differentiation than LD or ED classes. Now Jim walks in, and all my attention shifts to this guy.

Jim: large (not tall), bi-racial, 13, history of problems since kindergarten. I'd heard about him in the teacher's lounge. That's all I knew at this point, but for now I had to do something without knowing a whole lot else. So, I looked at the pass, looked up at Jim, and said calmly, "Thanks for coming with the pass. Please have a seat at the study carrel" (where my students and others sit for time-out). "I'll come over to speak with you in 5 minutes." Jim did not seem to hear me and kept tiptoeing around the room, grinning. I went over to him and asked him again to sit, saying that I would like for him to choose this as his time-out rather than go to the office. To my amazement, Jim kept grinning but complied immediately, although he did decide to tiptoe over there while looking at the other students with his grin to try to get their attention. What a great class I had! A few of my students looked at Jim but went right back to what they were doing. It's taken one semester to get these guys on board with what goes on in the classroom, and I think they would rather not have anyone tip the scales of our class structure, even if they would not describe it like that! I've learned that most students really crave the kind of organized learning environment we've set up, and once they're in the groove they're not too keen on having it disrupted.

They didn't have long to wait for it to blow up this year. Let me catch you up on the details: Jim left calmly after this time-out, without really saying a whole lot or interacting with me except through that odd grin and a few nods. His teacher and the administration must have been really impressed by this non-event, as the next week I was called into the office by the principal for a meeting:

Principal: Mrs. Lane (Stacey): "Well, Freida, I hear you worked wonders with Jim the other day."

Frieda Bailey (Me): "I don't know about that, Stacey. It was just another day in math paradise for me, and in comes a time-out kid. It wasn't much different from any other day."

Stacey: "Well, let me get to the point. Jim has had an incredibly tough year. He's classified SED [seriously emotionally disturbed], and he is going to more than one teacher for the first time since he entered school. The problems are occurring everywhere, and his modified-self-contained teachers have had it with him. We just added that SED self-contained class this year for those other guys, and I would suggest it for Jim, but we all think he would just go the wrong way with those street-wise guys in there now. So . . . what would you think about having him placed with you? His mom . . . "

Frieda: "Wait a minute, Stacey! My class is MiMH, and as far as I know this kid is strictly SED."

Stacey: "Yeah, but we are lucky that you have endorsement in all areas! With your structured class, I think this would be the best place for Jim that we have in the building."

Frieda: [I really don't remember what I said here, but I'll try to remember.] "Is there a meeting to discuss this more formally? I'd like to hear more before I can agree with that. I'm not saying I won't take him, but . . . "

Stacey: "Good. So, there is a meeting this Thursday. He's coming off a nine-day suspension to return to school, and his mom has been asking if he can be in some other class. She's threatened to sue at central office, and has been saying that she liked the homebound teacher so much, isn't there a way he can stay at home and get one-on-one instruction, or have someone with him all day here? We're going to go round and round on this one, if we don't respond. I don't want to bend to mom's whim, especially as she's claiming that the reason he doesn't do well is because he is African-American and the teachers are prejudiced. Thanks for considering the change to your class."

Well, needless to say I was no less comforted after this final series of information than I was with the first proposal that he join my class. So many questions came to mind: Is this the right placement for this kid, even if he did respond to structure? Would he get the services he needs, just because I'm endorsed, though the classroom and other students are so different? Do I want to have this family's concerns about fair treatment shifted from where they are now to me? And, I must confess, will this make my life miserable and ruin the careful, constructive balance already in the class?

You know how these things happen: Of course, Jim ended up in my room, and I had one day's notice to get ready. At the meeting after his suspension, it was decided that he could return to school, begin going to my class, and there would be a formal re-evaluation to determine his eligibility again—apparently, the school psychologist believed that Jim could, in fact, be EMR, as his IQ scores have been different each time he was tested and, therefore, there is some question about his actual ability levels.

I told the class, as soon as I knew he was joining us, that we'd have a new student the next day. "Who is it?" "Do we know him?" "He in this school, Ms. Bailey?" When I told them that yes, he is in this school and named him there was a cacophony of "Aw, man," "I *hate* that kid!" "That Jane's cousin!" "My stinkin' cousin in here! *No!*" Well, here we go, I thought.

Jim came to class that next day, and it was really awful. I gave him a seat in the front of the room, and he was so disruptive (turning around, making noises, wrapping his gym shirt around his head) that I moved him to the study carrel. "Until you can learn the rules of the class and feel comfortable enough to sit in the group," I told him. Maybe this was a mistake. He's been with me a week, and it has been the worst of my teaching career. He does no work (which was one of the main reasons his mom wanted him with me; she claims he did no work before because it was too hard) and scribbles all over his pages or crunches them up and throws out the work as soon as he gets it. I try to balance ignoring with reminders of what's expected, but I'm getting exhausted. The other kids are ignoring him sometimes, but they're also asking, "Tell him to shut up, Ms. Bailey," "Why don't he act normal?" "Stop staring at me, you weirdo." If I stopped for every one of these interactions, we would do nothing all day. One of Jim's most typical behaviors (I'd heard from other teachers and was now seeing for myself!) is to ask for something, and continue to ask, persevering on this one idea until he either gets it or gets in trouble. Some pattern . . . maybe he learned this at home, but it is really ingrained now! He asked me (without raising his hand, during a lesson), for example, "Can I go to tell the counselor something? Can I go to tell the counselor something? I need to go. I need to go. I need to go. My mom says I can go. Let me go." This continued, despite my calm reminders that he needs to stay seated, raise his hand, and wait to be called on if he has something to ask.

I should have anticipated this, but it happened again, with someone who did not know this about him. He is on "escort" to lunch with one of the teaching assistants. She came one minute late to class, and he started yelling, "You're late! You're late! You're late!" She told him that she would not take him until he calmed down and stopped yelling. He continued, adding, "I'm going, you can't stop me. I'm going to lunch. I'm going to my lunch!" She stood up, ignoring him, while I was working with the other students. Finally, Jim, with his famous "in the zone" grin, said, "I'm going and you can't stop me," pushed the assistant in the shoulder as he went for the door, and ran out of the classroom. The assistant was in shock; I told her to document what happened, let the rest of the class go to lunch, and called the office to have someone find Jim. The principal took our records of the event and called the sheriff immediately. This school has always seemed to use the sheriff's office too much, but maybe my sense of what's serious is thrown off by my years in special education! The police officer had a talk with Jim and told him that if this ever happened again he would be looking at a more serious consequence. For this one, they decided to call Jim's mom, set up a meeting the next day, and talk about how to respond.

At the meeting, Jim's mom said that we all should talk with our "loud voice" to get Jim to stop something. She said that that is what she does at home. I had to step in here and tell her that that may be the kind of pattern that has set him up for this kind of behavior in the first place. She listened, but was obviously confused and frustrated by the situation. The principal decided that we should have the school psychologist meet with Jim and talk about the pushing event, to help gather information that would help in deciding whether or not the behavior was a manifestation of his disability or not. As soon as Jim's mom signed the papers, we called the school psychologist, and she took Jim out of the time-out room where he was "waiting."

Do wonders ever cease? While I was having an informal conversation with Jim's mom after the meeting, taking this opportunity to get to know her a bit more and to assist with what seemed destined to be a long relationship, I saw the sheriff's car pull up in the front of the school. Two officers stepped out of the vehicle. I found out that they were there for *Jim*! Apparently, while the psychologist was interviewing him about yesterday's event, he said, "OK, I'm done now!" and stood up to leave. She asked him to sit back down, telling him that they were not yet done. He said again that he was going to leave, she moved between him and the door, and he pushed past her (knocking her to the side) just as he had with the teaching assistant the day before!

I found all this out later. Jim's mom had left for home before the officers knew she was in the building, and before she knew they were there for her son again! I went back to my room and I looked out of the window, trying to reflect on the whirlwind of events. The last thing I saw before shifting my glance at that master's degree on the wall was Jim leaving in handcuffs. What are we—or, now, *they*—going to do with Jim? If I couldn't make it work, is there any place in this school system that can? Is it too late?

Questions for Reflection

In what ways was it appropriate and in what ways was it problematic for Frieda to let her classroom be used as a "time out" for students in other teachers' classes? (Hallahan & Kauffman, Chapters 2, 5, and 8)

In what ways was Jim's placement in Frieda's classroom a good idea? In what ways was it a bad idea? (Hallahan & Kauffman, Chapters 5 and 8)

What do you think the school should have done with Jim?

What do you think law enforcement should do with Jim?

How do you think school personnel should have responded to Jim's mother's recommendation that they talk to Jim using a loud voice? (Hallahan & Kauffman, Chapters 3 and 4)

In what way(s) do you think the issues about Jim's behavior are culturally based or are related to cultural diversity? (Hallahan & Kauffman, Chapters 3 and 8)

How Did We Miss Jack All These Years?

Ginny Johenning

I have been a teacher for over ten years, beginning my career as a pre-school teacher, then a first grade regular classroom teacher, and then a high school special education teacher for students with learning disabilities and emotional/ behavioral disorders. Over the years I have encountered a number of students, too many really, whose lives have tugged at my heartstrings. After more than 10 years of working with kids, I believed that I had seen or at least heard just about everything. Then came Jack.

At the time of his referral, Jack was 15 years old, repeating the 9th grade, and receiving failing grades in most of his classes. The referring teacher said that Jack regularly entered her class in "crisis mode," pacing back and forth in clear distress. Many times, she wrote, this was in response to his younger brother, Drew, who was receiving special education services as a student with a learning disability. Drew was frequently removed from his 4th period special education class because of inappropriate behaviors and placed in the hallway near Jack's classroom. Jack would then feel compelled to talk with Drew in an effort to keep him from getting into more trouble. Jack would mutter, "there is going to be trouble" if he was not allowed to calm Drew down.

In addition to worrying about Drew, the teacher wrote, Jack also frequently placed himself in the middle of other students' problems and had difficulty leaving the stress of these situations outside of the classroom. Every day when he arrived in class, he asked to go see his guidance counselor or to attend mediation or to go to the attendance office or to go see one student or another because so-and-so was gossiping about someone else. She indicated that Jack had not had any major outbursts in class, but if his requests were not granted immediately he would become frantic and begin cursing to himself.

The referring teacher also described her various attempts at resolving Jack's problems. In an effort to redirect his anger or alleviate his worry, she reported, she would converse with Jack in the hallway nearly every time he came to class. She reported that he was fairly responsive to this "positive attention" but it would only "work" temporarily, as he would usually feel the need to stay in the hallway a little longer or go to guidance following these talks.

The teacher reported that she and the collaborative special education teacher, who was also in the classroom, would allow Jack a little more freedom of movement than the other students in the class. She stated that for the benefit of the rest of the class if Jack chose to disengage from the lesson by lying on the sofa and feigning sleep, then the teachers would respect his choice.

The referring teacher also wrote she had talked extensively with Jack's guidance counselor as well as with the administration. Her referral was a direct result of those conversations.

After receiving the referral form and prior to convening the initial Child Study meeting, I completed a review of Jack's school records and found some shocking information. Jack, in addition to failing the 9th grade during the previous year, had also not passed the state's standardized literacy tests, which students are expected to pass *before entering* high school and are required to pass *before graduating* from high school. He also had failed to pass any of the standardized End-of-Course exams administered by the state in the 8th and 9th grades, which students are required to pass in order to receive a regular high school diploma. Jack's discipline record was also extensive. We were only in the second month of the current school year, but Jack had already been in in-school suspension for 4 days and on out-of-school suspension for 4 days. No information was provided in the records about his specific offenses, but teacher reports indicated that Jack had problems with profanity, noncompliance, tardiness, and skipping classes. The records also indicated that Jack had been having behavioral problems in school since the 4th grade.

After receiving a referral on a student, I was required to schedule an initial Child Study meeting within 10 administrative days. Because this referral had been initiated at the request of the school administration, and because this student seemed to be having significant problems in school, I expected there would be an impressive turnout of school faculty and administrators at the meeting. For this reason, I was quite surprised that this Child Study meeting had to be tabled because the Assistant Principal, the parents, the school psychologist, and the referring teacher all failed to make an appearance.

Following this tabled meeting, my attempts to contact Jack's parents met with consistent failure. Jack continued to be suspended from school for various behavioral infractions. Finally, the administration required one of Jack's parents to accompany him to school for a re-entry conference before allowing him to come back to school following an out-of-school suspension. When Jack's mother came to school with him, the guidance counselor presented her with the form granting permission to evaluate Jack. Jack's mother, Ms. Shebly, signed the form without argument.

We then had 65 administrative days to complete the full evaluation on Jack and to convene an eligibility meeting. I was completely swamped with students who needed to be tested as part of their triennial evaluations, and the school psychologist, who would complete the cognitive testing component of the evaluation, was also buried in already existing work. Winter break was only days away, so we decided to start Jack's evaluation first thing when we returned to school from the break.

When we returned from break, we received some absolutely shocking news. Jack's younger brother had been arrested over the break and was being held on murder charges! The story we heard was that Drew and two other teenagers had traveled out of state over the holiday and allegedly had attempted to steal money from an elderly man. When the man refused to give them any money, they allegedly overpowered him and strangled him to death with his own shoelaces, then took his money.

Jack was tremendously upset by these events, of course. He blamed himself for Drew's behaviors and stated that if he had kept a closer watch on Drew none of this would have ever happened. The school psychologist and I decided to postpone administering standardized tests to Jack, as he was too upset for the results to be valid indicators of either his ability or his achievement.

Not too long after returning to school, Jack was in trouble again and was sent to the assistant principal's office. While talking with her, he supposedly became very upset and agitated and asked her if she was afraid he was going to strangle her. The assistant principal perceived this as a threat, and Jack was suspended from school indefinitely, pending expulsion.

The school principal instructed us to proceed with the evaluation right away. However, Jack was not allowed in the school building, so we had to complete our evaluations at the county administrative building. Ms. Shebly, Jack's mother, worked two jobs and was rarely home. Jack's stepfather, Mr. Shebly, had just recently been released from prison where he had been incarcerated due to assault with a deadly weapon. Jack's stepfather was also an alcoholic. His driver's license had been revoked following several DUIs. Transportation was a major problem for Jack. The school psychologist and I spoke with Jack's stepfather several times on the telephone and arranged for Jack to come to the office building to be tested. Mr. Shebly sounded intoxicated during all of these phone conversations. The school psychologist managed to complete the cognitive evaluation. However I did not have such luck. I arranged meetings with Mr. Shebly three times and, all three times, he failed to show up. The school principal would not allow me to go to Jack's home to test him because of the stepfather's history of violent behavior. During this time, Jack placed several phone calls to the assistant principal begging her to let him come back to school and apologizing for his behavior. He also called several of his teachers just to talk with them.

We finally decided to hold an eligibility meeting without standardized educational achievement information. The information we did have included a full cognitive and psychological evaluation and sociocultural information, including a great deal of Jack's family history. The psychological data indicated that Jack had average to above average intelligence, but a considerable amount of anxiety and depression, often manifested by acting-out behaviors.

The sociocultural information shed a great deal of light on Jack's problems. A county social worker went into Jack's home and interviewed his parents. What she discovered was shocking. Jack's mother was not his real mother, and this was information Jack discovered when he was 9 years old and in the 4th grade. He and his brother had been at a local swimming pool one day during the summer when they were 9 and 7 years old respectively. While at the pool, both boys were approached by a strange woman. She told them that she was their real mother. According to bystander accounts at the time, this information obviously upset both boys. When they began to argue with the woman, she attempted to hold their heads under the water, perhaps to drown them.

In fact, Mrs. Shebly confirmed that the woman at the pool was indeed the mother of the two boys and had been a former friend of hers. She had no idea who the boy's real father was, nor did their mother. The man whom Jack and Drew had believed for years was their real father was, actually, probably not related to them at all.

According to Jack, the Shebly's home life had been tumultuous as well. He had a vivid memory of his stepfather attempting to push him out of a moving car when he was a child, and he appeared to be haunted by this memory. According to social services records, the Shebly's home had been investigated on several occasions by a social worker, but nothing was ever reported to be amiss. Jack's difficulties in school began in the 4th grade and seemed to worsen as he became older. I wonder how so many adults in the schools and in the community could have missed the obvious suffering of a child for so long.

Questions for Reflection

Should Jack have been identified as having a disability? If not, why? If so, what disability and on what grounds? (Hallahan & Kauffman, Chapters 1, 2, 3, 7, and 8)

If you think that Jack had a disability, at what point in his school career do you think it could have been or should have been identified? (Hallahan & Kauffman, Chapters 2 and 8)

If Jack had been identified earlier in school as having significant problems (or a disability), how might subsequent problems have been prevented? (Hallahan & Kauffman, Chapter 8)

How might the teachers and school administrators have responded differently to Jack's insistence on being involved in his younger brother's behavior management? (Hallahan & Kauffman, Chapters 4, 6, 7, and 8)

To what extent do you think Jack's and Drew's problems were due to cultural influences or to family issues? (Hallahan & Kauffman, Chapters 3 and 4)

More than LD

Erin Ireland

As I look back on my experience as a mother of a child with a learning disability and attention deficit disorder I have mixed feelings. I love my daughter, but I wished I could have seen the signs of her disability more quickly and done more to help her academically and socially.

We have three children, David, Michael, and Shannon. David is careful and sensitive. Michael is outgoing and talkative. Shannon was different from both of her brothers. She was a pre-term baby, but there were no complications. She seemed to have normal development–walked at a year, talked at eighteen months. However, she was more shy and moody than her brothers were.

When Shannon entered school, she began to struggle from the beginning of kindergarten. She was good at art, but did not excel at any other subject in school; she was also clumsy which was very different from her athletic brothers. She also did not have many friends. At home, we often had to remind her of what she needed to do because she was very forgetful. Many of her household chores were left undone. We thought she would just grow out of it.

Her learning problems, however, continued and first and second grade were disasters. We were very troubled and when report cards came home we would try a new technique or reward to help Shannon so that she would do better. Shannon had problems in virtually every academic area, but especially in reading and mathematics. In reading, she was painfully slow at reading even the shortest story. She often could not answer even the simplest question about what she had read. Mathematics was just as bad. She could not tell time and often forgot her addition facts, although we practiced them all of the time. She, however, was never a behavior problem. We didn't know what to do. Finally, at the end of second grade her teacher recommended that she be evaluated for a learning disability.

It was not, however, until Thanksgiving in third grade that Shannon was evaluated. My husband, James, and I met with a team of professionals who reported to us on Shannon's psychological, social, and academic abilities. It was decided that Shannon was eligible for special education because of a learning disability. Her IEP stated that she would receive instruction for language arts and mathematics in the resource room for 2 1/2 hours every day, five days a week. We were unsure at first whether she should spend so much time away from her classmates, but over time we saw the value of intensive instruction that met her needs.

Shannon's special education teacher from third to fifth grade was Peter Martens. He had received his master's degree in special education and had been teaching for seven years. He made us feel at ease and encouraged us that students like Shannon could succeed. He taught students with learning disabilities in a resource room called the Learning Center. Mr. Martens worked with Shannon in the resource room for 1 hour and 45 minutes for language arts and 45 minutes for mathematics, besides giving support to her social studies and science work in general education class.

At first, Shannon was very shy and spacey and seemed to do no better in the resource classroom than in the general education classroom. Nevertheless, Mr. Martens kept working with her daily on phonics and writing exercises, keeping her engaged in instruction, making her work hard, and not letting up. He also worked with her in a small group for mathematics. In the Learning Center, her daily routine rarely changed and she had intense one-on-one instruction constantly. Mr. Martens made her work challenging and didn't let her quit. Then she started to catch on and was feeling better about herself. By early spring, she was learning like a real champion.

Mr. Martens told her, "School work is hard by itself. You're just going to have to work harder on some things. Just like some people would have to work really hard on drawing, but drawing is easy for you." Shannon also made friends with the other students in the Learning Center and learned how to help some of the younger students. I think Mr. Marten's positive attitude was helpful to her.

After several years of Mr. Martens' intensive remedial instruction, Shannon learned to read and understand what she read, to spell reasonably, and to compose essays and poems. She even made a B in social studies one quarter. However, she continued to have trouble with mathematics, lagging behind her classmates. Also, she never completely broke out of her shyness, especially in new situations and was still forgetful, especially in unstructured situations. She continued to be an excellent artist, and we tried to encourage this talent.

There were signs, however, that even with Mr. Martens help there was more than just a learning disability involved. I remember a note from Shannon's fourth grade general education teacher, Mrs. Maxey, "Sometimes, Shannon is so lost in her own thoughts that it seems like she's daydreaming. And then at other times, if she's working in a group at one side of the room and somebody says something about let's say a planet or recess—or just says some word that sounds like a planet's name—she'll pick up on that and forget the lesson. I don't know how to help her pay better attention. I don't even want to talk about homework or the way her desk looks."

James and I were always very grateful to Peter Martens, Shannon's first special education teacher. Yet, even with all of the progress, we still thought we saw signs of something more than a learning disability. We would say that we needed to be more structured at home or that soon she would grow out of this phase. It became clearer that we were going to deal with these issues at home and at school for the rest of her schooling. We became more depressed about Shannon.

When Shannon went to sixth grade at Wilson Middle School, the transition was more than she or we as a family could bear. She was in tears most days of the week. She could not keep her homework written down and never knew when there was a test or quiz. She couldn't remember her locker combination. She worried about not being popular; she didn't have many friends. As we talked to our friends, we realized that this was more than the typical adjustment from elementary school to middle school that all kids experience. We were all very frustrated. The only consolation was that she had one period of resource support with Mrs. Morgan.

After the first three weeks of school, Mrs. Morgan called us up and asked if we could have a conference. She said she wanted to talk to us about Shannon and her performance so far. James and I had sat through many meetings in Shannon's academic career, and we approached this one with a great measure of hostility and frustration. We had done all we could as parents. We were not going to have the school tell us we were bad parents or that we did not discipline Shannon. James said, "We have a loving family. Her brothers take good care of Shan and have been patient with her. If they start down that "you should" path, I'll pull her out of that school and put her in private school."

As we entered Mrs. Morgan's room for the conference, I could tell that there was hope. I took a deep breath. Mrs. Morgan welcomed us and told us that she enjoyed working with Shan. She said that she had put some of her artwork on her wall. We laughed and said that we were running out of wall space in our home for all other creations. Then Mrs. Morgan suggested that Shannon might have ADHD. At first, we were in disbelief. We thought ADHD was a condition that boys had. We sometimes thought our son Michael had ADHD; he had been very active and talked out a lot in school. There could be no way that our little Shannon could have this problem. She wasn't "hyper" at all. However, Mrs. Morgan informed us that ADHD does not have to be the acting out type. She said that research had shown that many girls with ADHD go overlooked because of their relatively good behavior, while all along they're unable to focus on instruction.

After the intense frustrations of the first weeks of school and our renewed trust in Mrs. Morgan, we were ready to try anything. After all, we had always had a gnawing feeling that we were seeing something more but could not put our fingers on it. We decided to set up an appointment with our family doctor, Dr. Rodriguez, to talk about the possibility of Shannon having ADHD. First, she gave Shannon a medical exam, and then we had a clinical interview with Dr. Rodriguez. Then she sent rating scales for Shannon's teachers and James and me to fill out. When we returned to the doctor, she reviewed the scales that we had filled out and the ones that Shannon's teachers had filled out. It was amazing to see the similarities.

James made the following remarks: "We were sitting with our family doctor, Dr. Rodriguez. She was asking us all these questions about Shannon's behavior, like did she have trouble focusing on homework, was she disorganized, was she forgetful? Then she had us fill out this checklist of behaviors. The more we talked about Shannon, the more I came to realize that I had always had pretty much the very same problems. It was as if a light bulb went off in my head. I could have been diagnosed with ADHD."

As we reflected on our conversation with doctor, we began to make other connections. We talked about how Shannon had always had a problem with either very positive or very negative news. We talked about how we cannot surprise her with good news. Just last month, when we were out to dinner at a nice restaurant, I wanted to tell her that I had found out that afternoon that her best friend, Marcia, was inviting her over for a sleep-over the upcoming weekend. I knew that I couldn't tell her while we were eating because she would likely explode with joy and embarrass us all. I had to wait until we were in the car on the way home. And of course, we all got to be the recipients of her ear-splitting glee. We talked also about how she reacts to bad news. Her temper can really flare up if she thinks you've wronged her in any way.

The results of the findings showed that Shannon did have ADHD, but the non-hyperactive type. All the signs—the inattentiveness, the lack of focus, the disorganization—were there since well before the time she was diagnosed. I think it was because she already had a learning disability. We thought that was what was causing all the attention problems.

We wondered whether Dr. Rodriguez would recommend putting Shannon on medicine. Actually, she recommended that we talk with her special education teacher first. We met with Mrs. Morgan and worked out several changes with Shannon's teachers. The first approach she recommended was to use a self-monitoring technique.

Julie Borne, her sixth grade math teacher, was skeptical of using this approach. She was having an extremely difficult time getting Shannon to finish her worksheets in mathematics. So long as Mrs. Borne was nearby she was focused; once she left, Shannon would daydream.

Shannon was supposed to record how she did on a sheet every time a small beep went off. The self-monitoring procedure worked almost from the very beginning. After Shannon used it for a month, she didn't need it any more. Mrs. Morgan also worked with Shannon's teachers to provide more structure so that she would not be lost. Teachers had set particular days for tests or quizzes and finished assignments were to be placed in certain places.

Mrs. Morgan also had a daily checklist for homework that Shannon had to fill out for the week and for each day. Because there were other students in Shannon's classes who needed extra help, the changes were not dramatic or ones that brought attention to her.

Even with all of the changes Mrs. Morgan had helped make for Shannon, she still experienced some problems with disorganization and day-dreaming. When we met with Mrs. Morgan to talk about these problems, she asked whether we had talked with Shannon's doctor about the possibility of medication.

At first, James didn't like the idea, but Mrs. Morgan reminded us that ADHD was more than just a behavior issue; it had to do with the brain and the way it worked (or, in Shannon's case, didn't work). So we talked the idea over with Dr. Rodriguez and concluded that it was worth a try. The results from the medication were obvious from day one. Shannon felt better about herself too and felt she had control of her life for the first time.

Shannon is fourteen now and in the eighth grade at Bishop Memorial Middle School. Things have gone better for her since finding out about ADHD. Shannon is also able to have more control over her disability. School is still a struggle for her, especially math. She can do her basic facts pretty well, but it's all gotten a lot harder with algebra coming on. However, she is turning in her work on time and is feeling more successful about school. She has more friends and feels better about herself. We want her to be able to get a diploma and go on to college so we're keeping with it. We want to have high expectations, but ones that are not unrealistic.

Shannon says, "My parents and teachers have always said that if I work hard and don't give up, I can be pretty much be anything I want to be. I've wanted to be a teacher since I was in second grade, but when I met my friend Ashleigh and found out her father works at the local TV station, I think that it would be fun to be a reporter on TV. I'm not sure. I want to work with famous people. I want to do something with my art."

Questions for reflection:

Why are learning disabilities and attention deficit hyperactivity disorder hard to separate? (Hallahan & Kauffman, Chapters 6 & 7)

What might Mr. Martens have done to make the transition to middle school less traumatic?

How are Shannon's father's remarks revealing in this case?

What about medication for Shannon? Do you think she would have been able to be successful in school without medicine? Was it appropriate for the teacher to introduce the idea of medication? (Hallahan & Kauffman, Chapter 7)

What characteristics did Mrs. Morgan see in Shannon that led her to think she might be a student with ADHD? (Hallahan & Kauffman, Chapter 7)

How might home and school have worked together during first and second grade when Shannon was struggling? (Hallahan & Kauffman, Chapter 2)

Where do you foresee Shannon after middle school? Do you think she will go to college and work in TV?

The Red Belt

Cindi Peterson

Tyler is a 15-year-old 10th grader. He began receiving special education services in 2nd grade, when he was found eligible and identified as developmentally delayed and emotionally disturbed. His reading and writing are well below grade level. When Tyler feels he is unable to do assigned work or is frustrated, he acts out. Ms. Peterson, his special education teacher, has seen many of Tyler's inappropriate behaviors. Extremely explosive, Tyler can suddenly become verbally abusive as well as physically agitated. He has never tried to hurt anyone in the classroom, but he sometimes stands up unexpectedly, pushes books and papers away from him, or walks out of the room.

Recently, however, Tyler has been doing quite well in a Work-Study program. He works at McDonald's in the afternoons and spends the mornings at school. Due to his behavioral improvement, Ms. Peterson recommended that he try taking one class in general education.

During Tyler's last IEP meeting, the IEP team decided that Tyler should start attending a general education math class. Math is a relative strength for Tyler because he does not have to do much reading. Although he had not been receiving the regular math curriculum in the special education class, Tyler's IEP team believed he could succeed in the general 10th grade math class. Since joining the math class, Tyler has appeared to be adjusting well. He attempts most of the math class assignments but does not usually finish them. He has been behaving appropriately in this general education class.

The other students in Tyler's classes both respect and fear him. He has the reputation of being a tough guy and someone you don't mess with on the streets. He spends most of his time on the streets and with his "homies." Tyler is very involved with his gang, but that relationship has interfered with school only once during the current school year. In early September in Ms. Peterson's self-contained reading class, Tyler wore a red sweatshirt (signifying gang identification). After a short and nonconfrontational private conference in which she simply asked him to take it off, he complied. There have been no more instances of gang-related behavior since then—until now.

On December 3, Tyler was in his third-period math class, the class immediately before lunch. Ten minutes before the bell was going to ring, Mrs. Collins, the general education math teacher, was talking to the students about what they were planning to do for the weekend, and most of the students were engaged in conversation about a current movie they wanted to see. Tyler was in the front row standing up and leaning casually against a desk with both his ankles and his arms crossed. Prior to this incident, Tyler had not been confrontational with Mrs. Collins. He seemed to be listening intently to the conversation but was not contributing much himself. Mrs. Collins tried a couple of times to pull him into the conversation, but from experience knew that when Tyler didn't want to talk it was better to leave him alone. While another student was telling the class about the movie, Tyler said, "Hey, Mrs. Collins." Mrs. Collins looked to see what Tyler had to say, but instead saw that Tyler had pulled up his oversized sweatshirt enough to expose a bright red belt with a gang symbol on the buckle.

Mrs. Collins said in a neutral voice to Tyler, "You need to put your shirt down Tyler, nobody wants to see that." Then Mrs. Collins started to walk toward her desk. On her way, she passed Tyler. As she passed him, Tyler turned to face her and said, "Look Mrs. Collins, it's *red*."

Mrs. Collins replied, "You know you aren't allowed to wear red at school. Now that you have shown me, what is it you would like me to do?" Tyler only stared at her.

Mrs. Collins knew the school's policy: Any gang-related articles of clothing had to be removed, and if they could not be removed, the student would be sent home via the office. She said, "Well then Tyler, you need to take the belt off and give it to me. I will hold it for you until the end of the day." Tyler took the belt off, removed the engraved buckle, and handed her the belt.

As soon as Tyler did this, the problematic situation became apparent to both him and Mrs. Collins. His pants were about four times too big for him. This meant that without a belt, Tyler's pants would fall off. Tyler was holding his pants up with both hands, looking down, and shifting his weight from side to side in the place where he was standing. Mrs. Collins opened her desk drawer and said, "Thanks for taking the belt off, Tyler. Let's see what we can do to help keep your pants up. How about a couple of safety pins?"

Tyler looked up at her, paused for a second, and then shook his head no. Mrs. Collins then said, "You could pin both sides, and when you pull your sweat shirt down nobody will be able to see them." Still Tyler shook his head side to side as he fidgeted in his place. Mrs. Collins suggested that he take the pins and goes to the bathroom. Still, Tyler just looked intensely down. Mrs. Collins found some twine in her desk from a science activity they had done and offered this to Tyler to tie around his waist. Still he gave no response. So Mrs. Collins said, "You can't walk around for the rest of the day holding up your pants. You will need to choose how you want to solve this, Tyler. You can either choose something I have here in the classroom, or you can walk up to the office with a referral to see if they have another belt you can use for the day." Still, Tyler gave no response. "Tyler," Mrs. Collins continued, "you really need to make a decision." As Mrs. Collins gave Tyler some time to think about it, he mumbled something under his breath and headed to the door.

"Are you sure you want to do that?" asked Mrs. Collins. Tyler stood by the door waiting for her to write the office referral explaining the situation. Mrs. Collins finished the referral, and as she handed it to him she tried one more time, "Are you sure, Tyler, that you want to take this out of our class-room?" But Tyler stood his ground. Mrs. Collins opened the door for him and watched him walk silently to the staircase. Then she went back into her classroom to sit down.

The other students started talking again quietly amongst themselves waiting for the bell to ring. Mrs. Collins used her classroom phone to call Ms. Peterson, the special education teacher. Ms. Peterson left her class in the charge of her assistant and walked to Mrs. Collins' room to get the full story. Just as Ms. Peterson entered Mrs. Collins' room, an office aide suddenly appeared at the door out of breath. "Tyler really blew it," the aide said. "We were waiting for the assistant principal and Tyler took off. It was like he just couldn't take it anymore."

"Which way did he go?" asked Ms. Peterson. The aide told her, and Ms. Peterson rushed down the hall and headed toward the front of the school to follow Tyler. When she walked out the front doors, she saw Tyler off to the right. He was heading away from the school. "Hey Tyler," she called, "I'd like to talk to you for a second before you go." Tyler looked back, and then turned around and headed back toward Ms. Peterson. As he approached her, she backed up so that they would be inside the front doors. The hallways were quiet, but she knew it was only a matter of seconds before the bell would ring. Tyler stood with his back to the wall, one hand in front holding up his pants, and stared down at the floor. "Are you all right, Tyler?"

"Yeah," he mumbled.

"That got a little bit bigger than you thought it would, didn't it?" Ms. Peterson inquired. Tyler just stared at the floor. Just then the bell rang to end classes and the hall started to fill with students. A friend of Tyler's came around the corner and stopped.

"Hey man, what's wrong?" his friend interrupted.

Tyler looked from his friend to Ms. Peterson, and with his free hand, shoved Ms. Peterson so hard that she fell backwards and hit her head on the doorframe. Tyler paused for only a moment as he met Ms. Peterson's eyes, and then sprinted out the doors of the school.

Tyler is now up for long-term suspension for assaulting a teacher.

Questions for Reflection

How do Tyler's characteristics fit the description of ADHD, and in what ways is his behavior like that of students with emotional or behavioral disorders? (Hallahan & Kauffman, Chapters 7 and 8)

What are the arguments for and against including Tyler in a general education class? (Hallahan & Kauffman, Chapters 1, 2, and 8)

Did the school over-react to Tyler's pushing a teacher, or should he be suspended for this behavior? (Hallahan & Kauffman, Chapters 2 and 8)

If you were to design an appropriate program of training and behavior management for Tyler, how would it differ from what is described in this case? (Hallahan & Kauffman, Chapter 8)

Should Tyler be disciplined under the rules that apply to general education students or under those that apply to special education students? Why? (Hallahan & Kauffman, Chapters 2 and 8)

How should Tyler's teachers have responded to his wearing gang colors in school? Did Mrs. Collins do the right thing by requiring Tyler to take off his belt?

How would you evaluate the way Mrs. Collins handled the situation after Tyler took off his belt and had nothing to hold up his pants? What else could she or should she have done?

Albert Says What?

Barbara Wing

I met Albert Roberts when he and his mother came to school during the teacher work week just before Albert started first grade. My first impression of Albert was that he was large. In fact, he was huge. Not only was he tall for a six-year-old, but he was also broad and pudgy—the kind of child that one of my relatives calls "squidgy."

Many new students are shy and quiet, but Albert fit the description of the strong silent male. When I spoke to him, he made eye contact, nodded his head yes or no, but he never said a word. He seemed curious about the curriculum materials that I showed him and his mother, and he smiled when I showed him which desk was his. But he didn't talk. He wasn't rude—he just never made a sound.

Before leaving, Mrs. Roberts said, "I don't think Albert should be a special education student, and I'll be anxious to hear what you think about him. He knows a lot for a six-year-old."

The information in the confidential folder said that Albert's receptive language appeared to be age-appropriate, but that he had a "severe/profound articulation disorder accompanied with a possible language delay." The final decision of the eligibility committee and Mrs. Roberts was that Albert qualified for services as a developmentally delayed student to be served in the class for students with mild mental retardation. When I called the special education supervisor for clarification, she said, "Mrs. Roberts specifically chose your class because you have a degree in speech pathology. She didn't care that you haven't worked as a speech-language pathologist for years. She just wanted a 'speech lady' to work with Albert every day." My supervisor also told me that some of the information about the educational assessment had been removed from the file at Mrs. Roberts's insistence. Specifically, Albert occasionally had violent, self-destructive episodes. He never attacked another student or a teacher, but he would throw himself on the floor or into the wall. Once, he slammed his pudgy body against the wall so hard that he cracked the wall board.

When school started, Albert seemed a model student. He participated in Direct Instruction reading, language, and math, which meant that he responded in unison with his group. I was never sure whether Albert's oral responses were correct, because his articulation consisted of grunts and strange vocalizations that I couldn't decipher. The other students may have thought his responses weird, but they never expressed their opinions.

Albert's speech may not have been decipherable, but his written work was beyond criticism. He correctly wrote his first, middle, and last name on every paper, even though only his first name was required. Every written response was correct and seemed to be professionally printed on the page.

We soon understood that any activity that required fine motor skills would occupy Albert for long periods. He copied from the board, wrote answers to questions from his reading lesson—sometimes in complete sentences—and spent free time writing, coloring, or drawing geometric designs that defied adult replication. But his favorite free-time activity was making complicated patterns with wooden mosaic pieces, and he was assisted in this activity by Ben, an autistic six-year-old who rarely talked. It remains a mystery to me how Ben understood Albert when he asked for a mosaic piece, but Albert would make a vocalization, undecipherable to anyone else in the classroom, and Ben would hand him the requested color and shape. Several times, Ben handed him the wrong piece, and Albert would shake his head, say, "Uh-uh," and then say something else, and Ben would always say, "Sorry," and hand him the correct piece. One of the other students found this amazing and would whisper to me, "How does Ben do that, Mrs. Wing?"

After a month, I thought that Albert had left his self-destructive ways behind, but then he showed me otherwise. He refused to do his reading follow-up one morning, and continued making mosaic patterns. When I told him that he would have to do his seatwork promptly or miss the extra recess, he gave me a dirty look and continued making elaborate patterns with the brightly colored wooden pieces. Extra recess time arrived, I refused to allow him to go out, and he threw himself onto the floor with such force that the ceiling light fixtures shook. After I took him to the school nurse to make certain that he hadn't broken any bones and called his mother to tell her that he might be bruised when he got home, I debriefed Albert.

I said, "Albert, you will not get your way here by throwing yourself onto the floor or into a wall. That scares me and the other children, and it's not safe for you to do that. Would you tell me why you did that?"

He frowned, his eyes got big, and he began to exclaim in unintelligible vocalizations. He gave me paragraphs of incomprehensible language.

Having no idea what he said, but aware that he was angry, I said, "I'm sorry that you missed your extra recess, but that was your fault."

He nodded his head. I continued, "If you throw yourself onto the floor or into a wall ever again, I will take away the mosaic pieces for two days. Do you understand?"

He began to yell in compound/complex gibberish again, but I held up my hand and said, "Yes or no, do you understand?"

He nodded his head, and I said, "Good. And please do *not* talk back to me."

As the year progressed, the speech-language pathologist and I worked closely, trying to improve Albert's articulation with little success. We knew that Albert had age-appropriate *receptive* language—he understood what someone else said—but neither the speech-language pathologist nor I could remediate his *expressive* language. Because his written responses were above grade level, we concluded that he was not retarded, and we wanted to find an appropriate placement for him for the following year. Mrs. Roberts was very cooperative and made an appointment with a doctor whose special-ty was working with children who had speech problems. In the meantime, Albert continued in my classroom with more mainstreaming in the regular classroom. At this time, the speech-language pathologist decided to teach him sign language, but sorting out language manually was just as confusing to Albert as speaking, so we soon abandoned that idea.

By Christmas, Albert's reading seatwork was so good that I moved him to a more difficult reading group. Much of the work was done in unison, but there were portions of every lesson when the students responded individual-ly. Whenever someone made a mistake, Albert immediately raised his hand to correct the mistake, and when I called on him, he always nodded his head, and said something. I never understood what he said; however I usually said, "Yes, that word is _____." When it was Albert's turn to read a passage, he always read. Even though I couldn't understand much of his oral reading, he answered his reading follow-up in complete written sentences, and he rarely missed a question. I began to provide extra seatwork for him because he loved doing it, and I could get a grasp of his reading comprehension. The speech-language pathologist and I thought that we might be hearing some vowel sounds in his reading, but there were precious few consonants, and his oral reading was still unintelligible. One person who observed Albert's read-ing group later asked me what language he spoke!

Albert continued to improve in academics, but socially, he was at sea. It's hard to form relationships if you cannot express yourself verbally and don't have the skills to write your thoughts. He played organized games dur-ing recess, drew, or played with mosaic blocks during free time in the class, but other than Ben, neither the students in my class nor the ones in main-stream activities approached him. The speech-language pathologist and I knew it was only a matter of a couple of school years before students would tease him about his speech.

One morning, I was teaching another group when my teacher antennae perceived that something was not quite right in the classroom. Ben was miss-ing. His mother was volunteering in my classroom, so I asked, "Where's Ben?"

"Oh, he left his snack in the regular class this morning, so I let him go get it."

"Oh, dear," I said. "I never let him leave the room without an adult."

"It's okay. I sent Albert with him."

My aide was already up, handing her instruction book to the student teacher, and we bolted out of the class. She took one end of the building, and I took the other. After a few minutes, we met at the library in the center of the school. We both had the same story.

"Those little devils have been to every class in that end of the building," she said.

"I know. They've darted into every class on the other end too. When I asked Betty if she'd seen two of my boys, she said, 'I don't know your students that well. But two little boys came in my class, laughing and talking funny.'"

We ran to the office, where Ben's mother joined us. The principal announced on the intercom, "Ben Thackeray and Albert Roberts, come to the office immediately!"

Sheronda, one of my older students also joined us. She said, "Ms. Wing, they were downstairs, too. Everybody saw them, but they're gone now."

"Okay now, let's not panic," the principal said. "We just have to split up and search outside. They're probably having a great time on the swings."

"I could think better," the secretary said, "if whoever is blowing that infernal car horn would stop!"

My aide and I almost knocked each other down running out the door. The boys were sitting in the P.E. teacher's brand new car, taking turns mashing the horn.

Ben's mother grabbed my arm. "You scare them. I don't care how you do it. But you put some real fear in them."

That wasn't going to be hard, because I was so mad at them that I could have ripped off the car doors. For a moment I feared that they had locked the car, but when they saw me they jumped out. I'm not sure what I yelled, but it was loud and long, and it momentarily petrified them. Then we formed up like recruits and went to the principal's office, double time! The principal did a good job of being stern with the boys. Ben was so awed at everyone's response that he became totally silent. Albert, on the other hand, wanted to argue with the principal. He growled and grunted, loudly protesting his punishment.

"You will not talk that way to adults, young man," the principal admonished.

He told me later that he had no idea what Albert had said. "But I know when I'm being cussed out!" he added.

Mrs. Roberts was angry that the boys had gotten away from us. I don't blame her. "Those boys could have gone down on 5th Street, and anybody could have picked them up!"

When I expressed the same worry to Ben's mother, she said, "Someone *could* have picked them up. But I guarantee you they would have brought them back in a hurry!"

Mrs. Roberts continued to take Albert to specialists: pediatricians, audiologists, speech pathologists, neurologists, and a myriad other professionals. None of them had even a vague idea of why Albert couldn't talk intelligibly.

In the meantime, Mrs. Robertson demanded more speech services for Albert—a request I fully supported. Albert participated in speech and language lessons three times per week, which was all the school system could handle due to both the lack of qualified speech-language pathologists and the lack of funds to hire more. Due to Mrs. Roberts's efforts and the efforts of other parents in my class, who petitioned local governing bodies for more money to hire additional pathologists, our school hired another speech-language pathologist, and Albert had speech and language lessons every day. Still, he showed little improvement.

By April, we knew that Albert was probably not going to speak intelligibly anytime soon—if ever. The only thing that kept Mrs. Roberts and me from openly weeping about Albert was his academic achievement. His math, reading follow-up, spelling, and handwriting were above grade level, and it was clear that he was not retarded.

In the spring, Mrs. Roberts asked the school to reevaluate Albert, and after all the tests were interpreted, she and the eligibility team agreed to return him to his neighborhood school with support services from the resource teacher.

When Mrs. Roberts and I left the eligibility meeting, she said, "You know my brother has the same problem. He never has learned to talk either."

I was stunned. How could an abundance of medical and educational experts, including yours truly, forget to ask Mrs. Roberts the important family history question of whether anyone else in her family experienced similar problems? I asked Mrs. Roberts's how her brother dealt with this articulation problem as an adult.

"Oh, fine. He finished high school, married, had kids, and he has a steady job. He doesn't work in the public because he still doesn't talk so anyone can understand him. I guess Albert won't either."

Questions for Reflection:

How would you classify and characterize Albert's communication problems in the light of chapter 9?

What do you think teachers or speech-language pathologists should do to address Albert's communication problems?

What evidence, if any, do you see that Albert had problems or disorders other than communication? (Hallahan & Kauffman, Chapters 8 and 9)

Do you think Albert should be receiving special education? Why or why not? (Hallahan & Kauffman, Chapter 2)

Had you been a general education teacher with Albert in your classroom, how do you think you would have taught him, managed his behavior, and fostered his relationships with his classmates? Whose help would you have sought?

Least Restrictive for Whom?

Mary Scanlon

At eighteen months old, Brian was diagnosed as severely hearing impaired when his mother pursued her concerns regarding his lack of speech development. Brian was her third child, and she knew the others had made many more baby sounds by this age. Money was tight in this working class family, but the children were properly cared for and a doctor was a necessity which they did not do without. Both parents had reasonably secure but low paying jobs in a factory in a small Northeastern city.

When hearing aides were prescribed for Brian, financial help was available from a local children's clinic. The local public school paid for Brian to attend a preschool for children with hearing impairment from the time that he was two until he was five. In that setting, Brian was trained to gain optimum assistance from his hearing aide and an auditory trainer, he was provided with individual speech-language therapy for 30 minutes three times a week, and he was taught a combination of Signed English and pidgin sign. After three years of these intensive services, Brian still had no understandable words. However, emphasis was still placed on vocalizing approximations of words, and he was required to vocalize as he signed.

The IEP committee, which included representatives from the public school, the preschool for students with hearing impairment, and Brian's parents, agreed that Brian would be placed in a local elementary school and receive the majority of his instruction in a self-contained class for students with hearing impairment. The teacher of that class would serve only one other student with moderate hearing impairment, who communicated orally. This other student received all instruction, except in language arts, in the general education setting. Brian would also receive speech-language services for 30 minutes daily. Despite the significant amount of service that Brian had received between the ages of two and five, the present level of performance statement on his first public school IEP stated that he was just beginning to understand simple questions such as, "What is your name?" It was reported that he knew manual signs for about 300 words, mostly nouns.

As the special education planner, I was the member of Brian's IEP committee representing the public schools. Although I had a master's degree in special education, I had never taken a specific course in hearing impairment. I did remember learning in my "Characteristics of Persons with Disabilities" course that deafness was probably the most difficult disability with which to live because of its affect on a person's ability to communicate. The only thought that I had given to deafness before taking that course was in playing the morbid childhood game in which we tried to decide whether, given the choice, we would prefer to be deaf or blind. I always chose blind because I was sure that my memory would suffice for my view of the world, but I couldn't imagine not being able to talk. So, with only my childhood bias for blindness over deafness and a few remembered lines from an introductory college course to guide me, I agreed with the recommendations of the experts who were present at the IEP meeting regarding the best program for Brian. I was proud that I worked for a school system that allowed a student who was deaf to be educated in a mainstream setting and felt that we were adhering to the guidelines for placement in the least restrictive environment as set forth in IDEA.

At this time, I was the only special education planner for a school system with 800 special education students. The job of chairing and completing the paperwork for all of the necessary eligibility meetings kept me in the office all of the time. I knew the students only through reviewing their IEPs, chairing their initial eligibility meetings (and then their triennial reviews every three years), and trouble shooting when complaints were made. I never had time to step inside a classroom to actually observe.

However, by the time Brian reached the second grade a new director and more education planners were hired, and I was able to begin weekly classroom visits to the four schools to which I was assigned. Brian's school was amongst those four, and I became the planner in charge of the hearing impaired program. On my first visit to the elementary classroom for children with hearing impairment, I became concerned at the extremely slow progress that Brian seemed to be making. My observation of his instruction revealed that Brian was still at a readiness level in all academic areas. His speech was completely unintelligible, and his ability to sign, with his teacher as interpreter, was sufficient for only very basic communication. I became concerned.

That same year (Brian's second-grade year), we hired Andy, who was himself hearing impaired, as a teacher of students with hearing impairment for the high school. He had been educated in a mainstream setting with hearing peers until graduate school at Gallaudet University. Andy's experience at Gallaudet changed his life and his philosophy, he confided in me. Having more time to concentrate on the hearing impaired program, I asked Andy to recommend some books about the education of students with hearing impairment. The first book he loaned me was a very dry college textbook. I kept it at my bedside from September until early December without getting past chapter one. I didn't want to learn to teach students with hearing impairment myself, I just wanted to gain a broad understanding of the methods available. Shyly, I admitted to Andy the problems that I was having in getting through the textbook. Just before Christmas break, Andy loaned me *Seeing Voices* by Oliver Sacks. This book proved to be very readable and incredibly interesting to me. It gave a clear history of the various and contrasting philosophies of Americans who are deaf. A pragmatist, I quickly took the side of those advocating manual communication. I read of the frustration of students of the oral philosophy, who might spend 10 years or more in learning to speak a few meager words, while students who are deaf educated in sign language from an early age had manual vocabularies equivalent to their hearing peers. Their reading and math skills more closely mirrored those of age-equivalent hearing students, while the academic skills of these students expending all of their energy learning a few basic words were far below that of age-equivalent hearing students.

I began to discuss my concerns about Brian's lack of educational progress with Andy. After five different observations in Brian's class, Andy requested a conference with me. When he suggested that I consider placing Brian in a residential school for students who are deaf, I was shocked. Although I recognized Brian's lack of academic progress, as a special education planner responsible for implementing the IDEA guidelines, I felt certain that a residential facility serving only students with severe hearing impairments could not be the most appropriate setting for Brian. Moreover, he was only seven years old, and he had a family who loved and cared for him, I protested. The picture in my mind of this residential facility was that of an orphanage from a Dickens novel—dark and dreary, providing minimal resources and stimulation.

A week later, Andy informed me that he had visited Brian's home. He observed a supportive home environment in which Brian appeared loved and accepted but was able to communicate only his basic needs through pointing and gesturing, as no one in his family had learned any form of manual communication. Although they insisted that they could communicate with Brian, it was apparent that this communication was in no way equal to the level of communication between his parents and a sibling who was three years younger than Brian.

I read more books about hearing impairment, I observed in the classroom, and I thought endlessly about Andy's recommendation for the residential school for Brian. Educational assessment at the end of Brian's second grade year revealed that he was functioning at the first percentile in reading, math, and written language according to an individually administered achievement test. His actual classroom performance was still at a readiness level in all academic skills.

Tentatively, I set up a meeting with his parents and mentioned the idea of residential placement in order to increase Brian's ability to communicate and learn. His parents were outraged at my suggestion, insisting that he was too young and that they would never let him live away from home. I was relieved at their strong opposition, because I was still certain that we were adhering to IDEA by educating Brian in the least restrictive environment—alongside his hearing peers—and that this was the best thing for him. When I met with Andy to tell him of Brian's parents' responses and my support of their responses, I saw anger spark in his eyes. I remember only one sentence Andy spoke in our meeting: "How can you consider this the least restrictive environment for Brian when he can only communicate with one person in the whole school?"

This question ran through my head like a mantra for weeks. All of the special education jargon and terminology could not adequately answer this one real-life question. In fact, he could only communicate with one person in the school, and even that communication was not adequate for anything but very basic dialogue. Brian was in a school of students with whom he could not speak and to whom he was, at best, that "poor deaf kid."

His parents, his teacher of students with hearing impairment, and his speech-language pathologist all agreed that the local elementary school was the best placement for Brian. I was becoming more and more certain that I could no longer support that view. I had to convince some of this group, most importantly his parents, that Brian needed to be immersed in a community that used manual communication in order to develop an adequate communication system. How should I do this?

The residential school was a hour's ride from the city in which Brian lived. Entirely fortuitously—and fortunately—I learned that a local church had a religious elementary school in the same town as the residential school. They transported their students daily. I had the idea of contracting with the church to provide transportation for Brian as a day student in the residential school. My special education director, aware of my concerns for Brian but unsure of the appropriateness of this segregated environment, gave me permission to approach the church with my request. I spoke to the school board, and they agreed to pay a reasonable fee for the transportation. I then met with Brian's parents to offer a day program rather than a residential placement. This time, at my request, Andy joined in the meeting.

Andy told Brian's parents of the strain of attempting for years to communicate with hearing peers and the joy he had felt when he was finally able to communicate entirely through manual communication. Although he was capable of satisfactory oral communication, manual communication was more fluid, not necessitating the intense focus required to speech-read, guess what the speaker said, and then carefully prepare each word of response. At Gallaudet, he finally felt that he was part of a community instead of an outsider. Andy's heartfelt story was the turning point for Brian's family. They admitted that they were becoming less able to understand Brian's wants and that they were witnessing more frequent displays of frustration and sadness from him. They would allow him to attend a residential school as long as he could come home to his family each evening!

That year I felt that I was sending three kids back to school in the fall—my own two and Brian. I spent so much time in the coordination of transportation and plans for the new placement that I was tempted to be there to meet the bus on the first day of school. I was as anxious as if he were my own! His mother and I spoke almost daily, and we shared our concerns about his going to this strange new environment an hour away from home. That hour ride would take him to another world, we knew. How would this seven-year-old who could barely communicate his most basic needs adjust in this new world? At eleven o'clock on the first day of school, Brian's parents were in my office. My heart lurched with fear when I noticed them. Then I looked more closely, saw their smiling faces, and relaxed as they hugged me. They had driven him to school that first day, and after his first hour at school he had smilingly told them to leave. He was already a new person, they shyly revealed. They had never seen him so relaxed and willing to try to communicate. In the course of his first hour he had gone from a timid, introverted youngster to a seven-year-old frolicking with his classmates, hands flying with their messages to one another.

By October, Brian was a residential student. His parents could not deny him the life for which he begged upon his return home each evening. They could not refuse their son the full life offered to him by this new school. With the help of the school social worker, they began to learn sign language so that they could communicate more effectively with Brian when he came home every other weekend. I visited the school and witnessed growth that seemed impossible after only a few months of schooling. The bleak picture in my mind was replaced with that of a beautiful campus full of smiling faces and flying fingers. My only sadness was that I could not understand the voices I could see.

Brian's latest IEP from the residential school (for fourth grade) shows him to be functioning just half a year below grade level in reading and to be on grade level in math. His mother and older sibling can now sign to him at home. And I have learned that the least restrictive environment, like so many things in life, is not always what you first think it to be.

Questions for Reflection

How should one interpret the notion of "least restrictive environment" in this case? (Hallahan & Kauffman, Chapters 2 & 10)

Mary Scanlon had learned in a "Characteristics of Persons with Disabilities" course that "deafness was probably the most difficult disability with which to live." Do you agree with this assessment? Why or why not? (Hallahan & Kauffman, Chapter 10)

At the first meeting with Brian's parents, they became angry when Mary suggested they consider placement in a residential institution. How might Mary have communicated with Brian's parents so that this meeting was more cordial and constructive? (Hallahan & Kauffman, Chapter 4)

Brian had floundered for several years in his neighborhood public school. Some, however, might consider the decision to make Brian a day student and then a residential student to have been made too hastily. What else might his teachers and parents have tried before making this placement decision?

A decision to place a student in a residential setting is never easy, and the timing can be particularly difficult. Assuming that the decision to place Brian in the institution was correct (i.e., in Brian's best interests), when do you think he should have been placed there?

The Reluctant Collaborator

Louise Gateway

I stopped outside the door of Ms. Cunningham's fourth-grade classroom to put my keys away and clear my head before going in. As an itinerant teacher for visually impaired children in a six county area, I visited several schools and classrooms a day and always needed a moment to make the transition from driving to teaching. When I glanced in the door, my heart sank and my blood pressure went up. Ms. Cunningham was in front of the room leading a lesson from a textbook, and every child had a book on the desk in front of him or her—except Pete. Pete, Ms. Cunningham's blind student, was sitting at his desk with no book, his elbows on the desk propping up his head with his fists pressed into his eyes. He was rocking slightly back and forth in his chair.

I took a deep breath and walked into the room. Ms. Cunningham looked up from her book with a big smile and a shrug, chirping cheerfully, "We couldn't find Pete's social studies book!" She continued on with her lesson, completely unconcerned, while I walked over to the bookcase holding all of Pete's braille books. Each print text that was transcribed for Pete took many volumes because of the bulkiness of braille, and the regional program I was associated with had supplied Ms. Cunningham's classroom with a bookcase to store Pete's books. There were probably 50 volumes representing all his texts, and each was labeled on the cover in print telling what book it was part of, which volume it was in the set, and which print pages the braille corresponded to. I looked at the print page that a student nearby had her book turned to and rummaged through the braille volumes until I found the right one. It was indeed slightly out of order in the bookcase, but it was certainly there and clearly marked. Ms. Cunningham smiled at me and shrugged again as I took it to Pete's desk and handed it to him. I whispered the page number in his ear, and he opened his book and found the place. Pete sat up straight in his chair, following the braille with his left hand while he raised his right hand to answer a question that Ms. Cunningham had just presented to the class.

I sat down in the back of the class with Pete's math notebook to inkprint the pages of homework he had done on his brailler the night before. Once I put the print translation above the braille on his papers, Ms. Cunningham could grade his notebook along with the rest of the class. Luckily, inkprinting took very little conscious attention because what I was really doing was seething and going over everything that had gone on between Ms. Cunningham and me in the past months, trying to figure out what had gone wrong with Pete's inclusion in fourth grade. This "Gee, no book!" incident was only the latest in a constant line of things preventing Pete from participating completely in Ms. Cunningham's class, and I needed to sort out the situation to see whether I was giving her too little support or whether she was taking too little responsibility for Pete's education.

First I went over Pete's history in Coolidge Elementary School. He moved to town the summer before third grade, and the advance information I received from his former school indicated that he was difficult to motivate and not up to grade level in braille reading skills or math skills. He had spent first and second grade in a self-contained class for students with visual impairments, but our region had no self-contained classes, using the itinerant model for providing services to children with low incidence disabilities. I had advised Coolidge Elementary that the best place for Pete was in a semi-protected environment for reading and math with mainstreaming into third grade for science, social studies, PE, music, lunch, recess etc. Pete spent third grade based in a learning disabilities resource room where the teacher and I shared responsibility for teaching him reading and math. The rest of his day was spent with Ms. Stephen's third grade. Pete really bore little resemblance to the child described on his IEP. While he had no terrific love for homework, he worked very hard in class and quickly came to grade level in reading and math. He had no behavior problems at all and was a popular student in Ms. Stephen's class. Unlike many of the blind children I had taught, Pete had no other "issues" besides his blindness and was a very "regular guy." Although the other third graders were initially curious and hovering, they soon accepted him as one of the crowd, and Pete had a number of good buddies by the end of the year. When we wrote his IEP for fourth grade, I saw no reason to have him spend time in a resource room, and he was placed in Ms. Cunningham's fourth grade classroom full time with itinerant services from me for 2 hours a day within the class.

My time in the room was largely spent transcribing worksheets into braille and inkprinting materials so that he would have access to everything presented to the class and so that the work he did on the brailler would be ready for Ms. Cunningham to grade. I was also there for math every day because so much of that was done on the board and I functioned as a board reader for Pete during that time as well as giving him tactile explanations of geometry, graphing and other concepts that were more visual than numerical.

I had expected a very smooth fourth grade experience, based on Pete's success in third grade and the fact that he had been so easy to fit into Ms. Stephen's class. The summer before fourth grade, I taught him to touch type and use a talking word processor so that much of his work could be completed in a format that the classroom teacher could read immediately. A computer and printer were placed in Ms. Cunningham's class for Pete's use, and he set up disks as "notebooks" for each of his subjects except math, in which he worked on the brailler. Pete was also provided with a computer at home so that he could do homework and hand it in in print instead of braille that needed inkprinting. All of Pete's texts were ordered in braille and arrived before school started. I spent five full days in Ms. Cunningham's class with Pete during the first week of school to trouble shoot classroom routines (How can he sign the lunch count board? Where will all his things be stored? How can he get the homework assignments off the board?) and make sure she understood his needs as a blind student. Ms. Cunningham smiled a lot, and I thought everything would be easy.

From the beginning, everything was difficult. The reading program at Coolidge Elementary was literature-based, and these books were not available in braille. I planned to braille the novels for Pete myself, but brailling a book takes about 10 minutes a page and I needed a lot of lead time to have books ready for him. I talked to Ms. Cunningham about this when we wrote Pete's IEP in the spring and she said she could let me know the first novel over the summer so I could have it brailled before school began in the fall. After that, I planned to stay a book ahead of him in my brailling. It took weeks to get Ms. Cunningham to decide on a first novel, but by the end of July I was brailling the book she chose and it was ready for Pete in September. Ms. Cunningham changed her mind at the last minute and started with a different book, not available in braille. She apologized and smiled and shrugged, but she wouldn't consider starting with the book I had brailled. She cheerfully warned me that "I don't usually plan very far in advance, and I change my plans a lot!" I started brailling the new book and managed to stay a chapter ahead of Pete for most of the book. His family read to him a print copy in the evening when my brailling got behind, but after spending hours and hours of my summer vacation brailling so that Pete could have a book like everyone else, I was disgusted that he and I were still struggling to keep up with the class assignments in September. I was never able to get far enough ahead of the class reading to relax, and it was a constant race to see if his next book would be ready before he needed it.

Ms. Cunningham wrote the daily homework assignments on the board before class started in the morning, and the students were expected to copy them down in an assignment notebook. I was not at Coolidge Elementary first thing in the morning to copy the assignments for Pete, and maximizing his independence meant having him do as much without my help as possible. Ms. Cunningham insisted that she didn't have time in the morning to read the assignments to Pete, so I suggested that she find a student who would be willing to read the daily assignment to Pete every morning while he brailled it on an assignment card. She agreed to do that.

One of the things that was starting to bother me was that Ms. Cunningham rarely approached Pete herself but preferred to talk to me about problems and have me deal with Pete. Several times a week she would complain to me that he had done the wrong assignments or not done some assignments at all. I started to check his brailled homework card against the assignments on the blackboard and found that he had copied many things wrong or left things off the card. At first, I fussed at Pete about this, thinking he was being careless or was trying to avoid homework, his least favorite activity. After a week or two I told Ms. Cunningham that he was making a lot of errors in brailling his assignments but that he had to take responsibility for being accurate and that she needed to deal with his missing homework the same way she would with any other student's. Pete spent many recess periods making up homework. Finally, many weeks later, Ms. Cunningham mentioned that the girl she had chosen to read the assignments to Pete had emotional problems and was purposely reading things wrong or leaving things out. Ms. Cunningham had suspected this for a long time but had let me continue to fuss at Pete and had let him do the wrong homework! She felt the girl needed something special to do and only reluctantly gave the task of reading to Pete to someone more responsible. Obviously, she didn't feel that it was important for Pete to have the work done correctly (although he was still required to do make-up work on his recess time), and this was a theme that continued.

Time for talking to classroom teachers is always short, so I set up a system in the beginning of the year that I had used in other classes to minimize the amount of class time taken up by my consultation with Ms. Cunningham. I needed to braille worksheets, handouts, and other short items before she used them with the class so that Pete would have his copy. I set up IN and OUT boxes on the window ledge where Ms. Cunningham could put things to be brailled and where I could leave the brailled copies for her to pick up and use. I included order forms she could attach to the print copies to let me know when she planned to use the material and any special format instructions.

Ms. Cunningham rarely left anything for me to braille. Instead, I would walk into class and Pete would be listening while everyone else followed or worked on a paper. Ms. Cunningham would look embarrassed, shrug and say, "I guess he needed a copy of this." By then it was too late to braille a copy for him. Every time this happened I explained to Ms. Cunningham how important it was for Pete to have the same materials as the rest of the class, and for a day or two she would try to have things for me to braille, but I always felt it was a token effort on her part. The situation always reverted to nothing in the box and nothing for Pete to read. At other times, even more frustrating, I would braille worksheets and Ms. Cunningham would forget that she had given them to me. Pete's braille copy would sit in the box while he sat at his desk with nothing to read. Several times I asked Ms.

Cunningham to set up just five minutes a day while I was in the classroom, during which she and I could touch base so that things would run more smoothly. She consistently and sweetly refused, repeating that she just didn't plan ve ry far in advance and everything was okay.

I suddenly realized while I was seething and inkprinting this day in February that the problem seemed to stem from the fact that everything *was* okay as far as Ms. Cunningham was concerned. While I was struggling to fit him into her class, she didn't think Pete really belonged there and was doing him a big favor by letting him "sit in." She probably thought she was being kind by agreeing to have him there. It didn't matter to her whether he did the work or learned anything because she didn't really believe that a blind person could be a part of society. I work with blind children all the time, and it had never occurred to me before that Ms. Cunningham might find Pete kind of "icky" and that was why she stayed away from him. Maybe she always managed to assign other students to explain things to Pete or trouble shoot his computer because she really didn't want to have anything to do with a blind person herself. I had dealt with hostile classroom teachers before, but it had taken me all this time to realize how hostile Ms. Cunningham was because she hid behind that sweet smile and shrug and always acted contrite. Although it was socially unacceptable for her to say directly that she didn't want Pete in her class, Ms. Cunningham never did anything to help Pete fit in, and she constantly set up roadblocks to his success. It was this indirect resistance that I was finding so hard to counter and accommodate.

I had to admit that Ms. Cunningham had not chosen to teach children with special needs as I had and that her unstated objection to having Pete in her class might stem from that. At the same time, I was furious that a child as easy to include as Pete was having a difficult time because he didn't fit Ms. Cunningham's picture of a fourth grader. I really believed that someone who called herself a teacher should be able to rise to the challenge of teaching *any* child placed in her class—especially with all the support she was getting from me—and I had seen many teachers do an excellent job of it after an initial reaction of fear and reluctance.

I had been struggling against Ms. Cunningham's silent refusal to include Pete all year, and now I wasn't sure there was anything I could do to change things. Confronting her with my new understanding of the situation seemed hopeless—changing attitudes about children with disabilities wasn't something that happened quickly—and if Pete's presence in her class and his obvious "normalcy" hadn't already won her over, then I didn't think there was much sense in a lecture from me. It was too late in the year to ask for Pete's class to be switched to another teacher, and Pete was happy with his friends. Maybe what I needed to do was lower my expectations for Pete and Ms. Cunningham for this year and hope for a more workable situation in fifth grade.

I really hated to admit that I was stuck, but it was something of a relief to understand what was going wrong. I also had a better idea of how important the individual classroom teacher was to the success of an inclusion situation. Pete's third grade teacher, Ms. Stephens, had sailed along with him with very little help from me; Ms. Cunningham wouldn't be able to make things work no matter how many hours I spent in her classroom or how many worksheets I brailled. I only hoped that I had learned enough from my experience with Ms. Cunningham about the qualities of a good classroom teacher to help me lobby for better choices for my students in the future. I was definitely going to be suspicious for a long time of teachers who smiled a lot.

Questions for Reflection

An itinerant model, by necessity, dictates that the special education teacher will visit the student with disabilities on an infrequent basis. What problems does this pose in this case? What are the implications vis-à-vis the least restrictive environment stipulations of IDEA? (Hallahan & Kauffman, Chapters 1 & 2)

As a general educator, what are Ms. Cunningham's responsibilities for accommodating the needs of a student with disabilities? (Hallahan & Kauffman, Chapter 1)

At the end of the case, Louise is determined to be more careful in the future with regard to the placement of her students with general education teachers. What do you think of this notion of placing students with some regular class teachers, while avoiding others? Does it violate the spirit, if not the dictates, of IDEA? (Hallahan & Kauffman, Chapters 1 & 2)

Successful collaboration between special and general educators depends on many factors. What factors might have made the collaboration between Louise Gateway and Ms. Cunningham more successful? (Hallahan & Kauffman, Chapter 2)

Louise and Ms. Cunningham were using peer tutoring as part of their plan for accommodating Pete in the regular classroom. How might they have implemented the peer tutoring more successfully? (Hallahan & Kauffman, Chapter 2)

This case, of course, is presented from Louise's point of view. To what extent do you think there is any possibility that Louise is to blame for the miscommunication between her and Ms. Cunningham? What could Ms. Cunningham say in her own defense?

Would more information about Pete's visual ability be helpful in determining the level of responsibility that Ms. Cunningham should assume for

his instruction? If so, what would you want to know? (Hallahan &
Kauffman, Chapter 11)

There is no mention of Pete's parents in this case. How might this information be relevant to deciding what to do on his behalf? (Hallahan &
Kauffman, Chapter 4)

Getting to Know Chase

George McKenna

The first thing I did, once my bags were unpacked and my new apartment was reasonably organized, was sit down and watch the video tape. Before I left the east coast to begin a doctoral program at a mid-western university, my colleagues and students had used a camcorder to record their goodbyes and well wishes. I had already seen the video twice before. The first time was on my last day of work with the entire school; this was possible because, as a center program for students with emotional disabilities and behavioral disorders, my school had only 25 students and 16 staff. As I sat at the front of the group, laughing and smiling at the video, I was unprepared for the strong emotions that welled up inside me. That night, I shared the video with friends at home. They, too, sensed the caring and community of this special school, captured so poignantly in a mosaic of touching and humorous moments. Now, surrounded by empty luggage and folded clothes, I watched it alone. The images and sounds swirled out from my television.

At the center, I was one of two crisis resource teachers. We shared a desk in a small crisis resource room, from which we developed and ran the center's crisis program. Our duties were twofold: we provided ongoing assistance for students who exhibited extreme acting out behavior, and we collaborated with classroom teachers to select and implement proactive strategies to prevent crisis and to teach students appropriate behavior and adaptive skills. In this role, I worked with all of the students and staff. For every face I saw on the video, I had memories of struggles and triumphs, frustration and growth.

Even against this background of intense emotion and experiences at the center, one student stood out for me—Chase. There he was, appearing in the video with the other four boys in Margaret Choy's fifth-grade class, saluting me with Ms. Choy's raucous classroom cheer. Where the other boys finished the cheer with "Mr. M.! Mr. M.! Rah! Rah! Rah!," Chase shouted "Mr. M.! Mr. M! Touch his beard!" I smiled when he did it; it was simultaneously so strange and so familiar. My friends had laughed when they saw it. They looked at me with amused and puzzled expressions. It made a little more sense if you knew Chase. And I had spent a year getting to know Chase.

I met him the first day of school as I made rounds introducing myself to each class (I knew it was important to build relationships with the students and teachers away from and beyond the chaotic moments of crisis). On the playground, Ms. Choy's fifth-grade boys sheepishly introduced themselves and spoke with me in a manner you'd expect of fifth grade boys. Without warning, Chase lurched out of the group and towards me, seemingly unaware of the nervous air that hung around the rest of us. He was large, heavyset, just an inch or two shorter than me, with glasses perched precariously on the tip of his nose. He stood uncomfortably close, and he peppered me with questions that would have made for excellent introductory small-talk, had they been delivered in a calm manner that suggested he was interested in my responses. The inflection of his voice was unnatural, flat and robotic for the most part, with exaggerated changes in pitch that made it sound like he was trying to imitate typical speech. My deft (or so I thought) attempts to rein Chase in and have a more normal, reciprocal interaction were derailed by his increasingly absurd questions about video game characters, bulletproof vests, and broken glass. Margaret swooped in and saved me in a way that indicated she had done so many times before. She slipped between us and prompted Chase to say, "Nice to meet you," after which he hurried off to play basketball by himself. I watched him play for a while. Between each shot he paced the court, rocking forward on one foot, and pulling his elbows back as he flapped his hands at his side. He would then take another shot and repeat the pacing. My sense was that if the all of the adults and children on the playground, with the exception of Chase, were suddenly sucked up by a tornado right at that moment, it would have taken Chase a long while to notice. He seemed oblivious to his surroundings.

Later that afternoon, I stopped by Margaret's room and we spoke about Chase. I had some experience with students with autism, but less experience with students with autism who are higher functioning. Margaret noted that Chase read and performed math operations at grade level and was stronger academically in some areas than the other four boys in her class, but he had difficulty with comprehension, writing, and word problems. "Chase's academic strengths present some real opportunities for him," Margaret said, pulling a worn file from her desk drawer, "but his behavior can be explosive. Elaine had him last year. She's probably the most patient and flexible teacher in the building but, well, as much as she hates to admit it, by June she was glad to see him go. I don't mean to make this sound negative, George, but I know that you and I will be seeing a lot of each other this year."

The next morning I skimmed most of the students' records. I read over Chase's diagnosis of autism, and I pieced together a sketch of his school history. In second grade Chase began the year in a noncategorical classroom in his neighborhood school, and even spent part of his day general education. However, over the first few months, his behavior deteriorated. He began throwing materials, stomping out of classrooms, shouting at other children, and screaming threats. By November, these outbursts had increased in frequency, intensity, and duration. At an IEP meeting in late December, the school team, including Chase's parents, agreed that Chase's educational needs could best be met at the ED/BD center program.

Elaine stopped by the crisis resource room after lunch, while her class was in the gym for PE. "Chase really can be a sweet boy," she said, "but there are certain phrases and sounds that really upset him. The word 'problem' upsets him. The sound of people clearing their throat. Oh, and 'uh-huh,' like when you say 'uh-huh' instead of 'yes.' Imagine trying to not say 'uh-huh' all day long. It's impossible!" We both laughed. "Oh, and the big one," her eyes got wide, "is 'don't do that.' Guaranteed, the desk is gonna be flipped over and we're going to be down here screaming."

Elaine pointed out that some of the other kids in his class would deliberately set Chase off by whispering one of the "trigger" phrases or words to him. Acting out students from other classes had tried to set Chase off from down the hall or while being escorted to the crisis resource room.

Despite the dire predictions, the first few weeks were pretty quiet at the center. The few students who did spend time in the crisis resource room were angry but in control, and I problem-solved with them to good effect. I was able to help out in classrooms, and I got to spend more time with Chase. I would occasionally sing rap songs with him on the playground, and he tried hard to memorize the lyrics, asking me to repeat certain lines over and over.

Chase displayed numerous idiosyncratic verbal behaviors. Whenever he heard a car horn from the street or parking lot outside, he would say "Pink Panther is squishing an egg." If he did not know the answer to a question he had been asked, he would never say "I don't know." He would begin like he was going to answer, as in "Twenty-four divided by six is . . ." But instead of finishing with the answer, he would say "Hawaii kee kee!" The other boys in Margaret Choy's class were so used to this that they would often join in with Chase, saying, in unison, "Hawaii kee kee" without looking up from whatever they were doing. I also learned that Chase was fascinated with broken glass. Whenever we ever went for a walk or out to the buses, he would scan the ground for broken glass. If he saw some, he would run over and stand close to it, sometimes bending over like he was about to touch it. He would respond immediately to adult requests for him to move away from the glass. Sometimes it seemed that what he enjoyed was the entire ritual, including the adult reaction at the end.

By the end of October, things had started to "heat up" in the crisis resource room. The younger students who were new to the program were apparently over their initial apprehensiveness, and a couple of them were having daily tantrums that lasted an hour or more. Jennifer, the other crisis resource teacher, pulled back from helping with administrative duties and resumed her partnership with me. We met frequently with teachers and seemed to be managing to resolve some of the more complex issues, one step at a time.

Then, one Friday in mid-November, just 30 minutes or so before dismissal, I heard an incredibly loud, piercing scream in the hallway. I raced outside and saw Margaret standing with Chase in the hall. Chase was ripping up papers and screaming into his classroom at someone I could not see. As I moved quickly and calmly to the other side of Chase, I saw Ms. Warren, Margaret's assistant, urging David, another one of Margaret's students, back into the class. David was grinning from ear to ear. Chase's desk was overturned, and materials were scattered around the entire room.

The screaming was so loud that it was impossible for Margaret and me to talk. Fortunately, we had planned what we would do if Chase became out of control the way he was at that moment. We gently took Chase by the arms and led him to the crisis resource room. Chase flailed around a bit, but he was generally allowing himself to be led, and he was far weaker than I might have guessed by his size. When we got to my room, Chase flung himself to the floor and began yelling threats at me and at David, all peppered with curse words. Margaret and I waited for Chase's verbal venting to subside somewhat, and then I directed him to a desk. He jumped up and fell into the seat, banged his desk with both fists twice, and sat huffing and staring, his face tense and red, sweat beading on his forehead. Margaret went back to debrief with her class, and I sat pretending to write at my desk, giving Chase enough time to calm down. Margaret returned and we decided to escort Chase early to his bus, which he rode with two other students and an attendant. When the bus pulled away, Margaret and I looked at each other, and I mouthed a silent, "Wow." She nodded.

Inside, she called Chase's parents and several of us met to talk about the incident and Chase in general. Near the end of our meeting, I asked about the parents and how things were at home. Margaret said, "Oh, Chase's parents are very sweet, and they try very hard. However, they don't go out much, and they spend most of their days trying to avoid setting off another episode. He does a lot more silly talk with them, because they play along a lot more than we do. He can get mad if you don't stick to his script."

Elaine added, "Last summer they took him to a clinic that claimed his problems had to do with how his brain handled auditory information. He spent several weeks listening to headphones, I think, and it cost a lot of money. Mom and Dad were really hopeful but, even though they were the last to acknowledge it, it didn't make any difference in Chase's behavior, at home or at school."

The next morning, Chase came directly to the crisis resource room and did individual work until lunchtime. He did not earn the points he normally earned while working in his class. This was in keeping with the way staff responded to serious outbursts the previous year.

Up until winter break, Chase had several outbursts a week. It seemed like the first episode started the ball rolling, and Chase was more agitated and on edge in general. We stuck to our program, trying to encourage Chase to ignore the words and phrases that upset him so he could earn points, rewards, and privileges available to him in class. I also spent more time with Chase in class, at lunch, and during recess, when he was calm. We sang rap songs, and I talked more to him about his "silly talk." I was able to figure out that Chase said "Pink Panther is squishing an egg" when he heard a car horn because he had once seen a cartoon where Pink Panther squished an egg and it made a honking sound. I also learned, with some careful questioning, that the word "problem" set Chase off at least partly because he associated it with a movie called *Problem Child*, in which the child lead engages in slapstick misbehavior.

It was also during this time that I saw how Chase engaged different center staff in person-specific ritualized interactions. For example, he would always go up to Mike Southern, one of the instructional assistants from another class and say, "Mr. Southern, stutter." To which Mr. Southern would respond, "N-n-n-n-no!" Chase would laugh hysterically. But he only did this with Mr. Southern. It was as if Chase navigated his social world through a series of rigid associations—words to events, interactions to people, actions to places. As frustrating as Chase's outbursts were, he was also a really interesting person.

Over winter break, besides resting and working up my second wind, I thought more about Chase, and hoped I could get everybody together to assess his behavior and modify our efforts to help him. The first week we were back, Chase had three major acting-out episodes. The third happened while I was in his class working with him in an effort to reduce the tension. To encourage him as he finally managed to read a particularly challenging word, I said, "Uh huh." He tensed in his seat and stared at me sternly, telling me not to say that word. After calmly prompting him to finish the passage, I decided the situation called for a strategic activity switch. "Let's go ahead and do some math problems," I said. Chase screamed at me, banged his book on the desk, and kicked the cart next to him. Margaret and I escorted Chase down to my room. Before she went back to her class, we briefly spoke and agreed to meet that afternoon.

Everyone at the meeting took a collective step back and did their best to take a fresh, objective look at what was occurring with Chase's outbursts. We noted that the episodes always ended with Chase removed from the room, away from the words or other stimuli that were bothering him. Also, Chase's behavior had had a significant impact on our behavior; that is, we made every effort to sidestep certain words and situations in order to steer clear of his rages. In the long run, this was not helping Chase. We decided that Chase needed to learn to deal with these things that upset him—first by learning to remove himself from the situation, and maybe later, given the reassurance that he had another option besides screaming or suffering the words that bothered him so much, he could find ways to cope without leaving. Finally, our revised plan called for a highly individualized system of positive reinforcement for refraining from his outbursts. Margaret spoke to Chase's parents on the phone later that night, and they thought the suggested changes made a lot of sense.

The next day I walked Chase through the steps of leaving the classroom when he was upset. He had his own red pass that he was to hold up as he left. Also, we wrote down the leave-taking routine as a series of concrete steps, describing when he might want to leave, what he was to do when he left, and how he was to return. Chase and I also selected some novel rewards to acknowledge his successful use of the new strategy. As a short-term (weekly) reward, I would record one of the rap songs we sang onto a blank tape supplied by Chase. For his first monthly reward, Chase asked if he could take Ms. Choy's shark poster home. We were surprised that he wanted it because he never gave any outward signs of liking it. The poster was inexpensive and, as Margaret put it later, more than a fair trade for a reduction in outbursts. Chase would get a song on his tape for accumulating five days with no outbursts, and the poster was his for accumulating 20 days.

The first week, Chase had no outbursts and left the room only one time despite, as Margaret pointed out, several utterances of "trigger" words. The first time Chase came down to the crisis resource room with his red pass, I praised Chase emphatically. He was tense, and he told me that he didn't like it when so-and-so said one of the words he hated. I calmly reminded Chase that no one was trying to make him mad, and he had to learn to deal with it. That was the overarching theme of the latest plan. Chase would have to learn to deal with the realities of the classroom.

At the end of the first week, I took Chase's tape home and happily popped it into my stereo. As I was cueing it up to dub the first song, I heard Chase's voice coming out of my speakers. He had recorded himself playing video games on the tape he had given to me. Chase was saying silly things in response to events on the video game and commenting on the actions of the absurdly named video game characters. Occasionally, he stopped the tape and spoke directly into the microphone, recording seemingly nonsensical, rambling phrases, apparently for him to listen to later. At one point, Chase recorded himself playing video games with someone who turned out to be his babysitter. As he played, he asked his babysitter to repeat strings of words and sounds, which she did. I ended up listening to the entire first side of the cassette, smiling at some things and shaking my head in wonder at others. When it was over, I flipped the tape and recorded one of my favorite songs, also one of Chase's favorites.

Chase did really well with the new plan. In fact, he went straight through the first 20 days without an outburst. There were some close calls. One morning David had to be escorted from the classroom, and he started yelling, over and over, "Don't do that!" at Chase, trying to torpedo Chase's recent success, which had garnered a lot of conspicuous praise and attention. Chase held up his pass and ran out of the room, past the crisis resource room, all the way to the back of the center office, startling the administrative assistant who was putting supplies in the storage closet.

Things generally went well through the spring. Margaret was able to work hard with all of her students, and there even seemed to be a ripple effect for the entire center, which seemed calmer and more positive. Chase did have more outbursts, but they were less intense and far less frequent. He had some trouble remembering his leave-taking routine in less familiar settings, such as other classrooms or during large group activities, like assemblies. We were all proud of our progress, nonetheless, and reducing Chase's outbursts even further seemed likely.

One day in late March, while shooting baskets with Chase, I impulsively asked Chase if he could feel the rough spot on my beard. As he moved his hand close to my chin, I suddenly barked and pretended to bite his hand. Chase laughed at my gag. The rest of the year, Chase would ask to touch my beard, and I would respond with my wild dog impression. To Chase, I had become the "touch the beard" guy.

In April I received an acceptance letter to a special education doctoral program. It was very tough deciding to leave this terrific program that was doing such important things for kids, especially after only one year teaching there. I knew it was the right decision, and people at the center encouraged me to pursue the advanced degree. And as a send-off, even though I felt like I had only been there for the blink of an eye, they had made this video that acknowledged my part in a truly special community, and allowed me to bring a little piece of it away.

I sat watching the final seconds of the video—a wide shot of the whole school on the playground, everybody waving and goofing off for the camera. Down in the corner stood Chase, rocking on one foot, looking at the ground. The questions raced through my mind: How would Chase meet the challenges of his life? Will Chase remember me, and in what way? How will others experience the challenges of getting to know Chase?

Questions for Reflection

In what way(s) do you see Chase's behavior as typical of the students described in chapter 12?

What do you think of the way George McKenna thought of and responded to Chase?

What do you think of Chase's parents' (as reported by Elaine) decision to have him listen to auditory stimuli with headphones? In what way is such treatment typical or atypical of students with ASD? Are there other treatments for ASD that you would put in a similar category as the listening treatment to reorganize brain function? (Hallahan & Kauffman, Chapter 12)

Chase was being taught in a special school or center. Do you think he should have been? How do you think he likely would have fared in a regular school? Why? (Hallahan & Kauffman, Chapter 2)

What do you think are the most important things for Chase and students like him to learn?

Who Will Help Patrick?

Candace Keller

The first thing that I remember about Patrick is Sara's story of how his foster mother refused to give him a taste of barbecue ribs as she sat hunkered over the table enjoying her large portion of the steaming pile while Patrick whimpered pitifully at her feet, begging for the taste he would never receive. Food used to manipulate and taunt is a thread running throughout Patrick's story. But I am getting ahead of myself.

Sara was at Patrick's apartment in a federally subsidized housing project to perform developmental testing as part of a large battery of evaluations which would be used to determine whether Patrick qualified for special education services from the public schools. Minutes after leaving the dark apartment, Sara sat in my office, enraged and in tears, describing the horror of observing the interactions between this two-year-old and his foster mother, Margaret. Never had Sara seen interactions marked with such extreme intimidation and so totally devoid of nurturance. Never had she seen a child so unable to relax and smile. These were the first of many tears to be shed for Patrick. And there will be more.

Patrick's birth mother, Debra, was a substance abuser who used both alcohol and drugs during her pregnancy. After Patrick's birth, she roamed the streets of the small midwestern city in which she lived, often carrying him with her and leaving him asleep in alleys while she used whatever was available to get her high. As one of the special education coordinators for the local public schools, I was familiar with her history because two years earlier I had chaired the eligibility meeting for her first child, Sade'. Sade' had been placed in a preschool class for children with disabilities because of her extreme behavior problems, but she was now in the custody of relatives in another state. I knew that before Patrick was born Debra had been taken by her social service worker to a clinic to be voluntarily sterilized but had left through a rear door before the surgery was done. The next time the social worker saw Debra she was visibly pregnant with Patrick.

Patrick lived for his first six months with Debra, who continued to live the life of a street person throughout that time. More than once he was found abandoned and screaming in some dark hall or alley. More than once in the first six months of his life he had to be treated for oozing staph infections on his head and arms. Finally, when Debra was sentenced to a short time in the local jail, Patrick was placed by social services in the home of Margaret, his current foster mother.

Margaret had been recommended to social services by Debra. Margaret, who had been a special education student and an acquaintance of Debra's, had four teenagers of her own and needed the money that social services paid to foster parents, meager though she alleged it to be. When I questioned the caseworker about the suitability of this home for Patrick, she countered with her own question, "Who else will take him?"

Patrick was referred to the public schools for evaluation by a public health nurse, who felt that he exhibited developmental delays. She was particularly concerned about his low weight and speech delays. At Patrick's eligibility, unlike any other that I had chaired in more than a decade as special education coordinator, each evaluator told a similar horror story of the terror that they felt from the somber, frail Patrick in reaction to the orders barked at him by Margaret. Each report reiterated how he sucked three fingers (calloused from the act) and rubbed his head with his other hand while Margaret insisted that he could do what he failed to do for the assessor. Only once, in five separately administered evaluations, did he smile—when he threw a ball which was caught laughingly by the evaluator, who praised his fine ball handling ability.

The results of all of the evaluations determined that Patrick was developmentally delayed and impaired in speech and language. The developmental assessment indicated significant delays in the areas of adaptive behavior, communication, and cognitive skills, with some delays in motor skills. The psychological evaluation noted that he had many features associated with fetal alcohol syndrome and that he remained apprehensive throughout the testing period. He responded quickly to inhibitions such as, "Wait a minute!" and acted fearful when Margaret spoke loudly to encourage him to complete a task. Unlike most 26 month olds, he did not respond differentially to praise or encouragement. The skills that he demonstrated placed him at the 19-month-old level, and the psychologist suggested that he appeared to be experiencing considerable sadness, apprehension about others' behavior, and a lack of self-confidence. The speech-language evaluation documented communication skills that were uniformly about one year below the expected level. Discussions with Margaret revealed that Patrick seldom initiated interactions and that when he did, it was nonverbal through pointing and vocalizing by crying. The speech-language pathologist found the extreme harshness of Margaret's interactions with Patrick noteworthy. The sociological evaluation, written after an interview with Margaret, stated that Margaret could benefit from assistance in teaching Patrick some developmental skills and in developing appropriate behavior management strategies. The medical evaluation revealed that, although he was judged to be healthy, he was anemic and his weight fell below the fifth percentile, as did his weight-to-height ratio.

When he was two years and five months old, Patrick was placed in a preschool class for children with disabilities with seven other youngsters served by an experienced preschool special education teacher and an assistant. He quickly became the most challenging student in the class, exhibiting severe mood swings from cooperative to belligerent, from loving to aggressive, from lethargic to tantruming. Patrick was invasive of other students' space, often hitting, pinching, and attempting to bite them. His need for food was often insatiable, with demands for food beginning as soon as he got off of the school bus. During his first year of preschool—February to June—his teachers attempted to manage his behavior by putting him in time out in a playpen when he was hyperaggressive. The entire school was traumatized by loud, piercing screams, sometimes lasting for more than an hour. Aware that the recommended amount of time-out for toddlers is one minute for each year of age, the teacher attempted to limit Patrick's time out in the playpen. However, his aggressive behavior and unwillingness to change often left her with no recourse but to leave him screaming wildly in his playpen so that she could attend to the other students.

The teacher approached Margaret for help in managing this behavior, which was totally unpredictable and seemed clearly out of Patrick's own control. Margaret was extremely critical of the teacher's techniques and offered the teacher permission to beat Patrick. When asked to visit the classroom, she grudgingly complied. Each time, her appearance in the doorway caused an immediate change in Patrick's demeanor, which became passive and withdrawn, three fingers going quickly into his mouth and the other hand rubbing his head vigorously. No inappropriate behaviors were ever displayed when Margaret was in the classroom. On one visit, when it was planned that Margaret would observe so that Patrick would not be aware of her presence, he suddenly and without explanation began to tantrum. Margaret quickly burst into the room. Upon seeing her, Patrick immediately stopped, fear etched upon his little, fine-boned face.

The thread of insatiable hunger, the thread of fear, the thread of intimidation were becoming apparent to all of us who were involved. We made more calls to social services; again, they asked their question, "Who else will take him?" Sickness gripped the hearts of those who cared. While we could not change the bad beginning to his life, this was a social service placement—this was supposed to be a better place than that from which he came! Something was wrong. The system was not working. What could we do?

In September, when Patrick was three years old, he began his second year of preschool. His aggressive behaviors escalated. He threw toys unexpectedly. He lashed out at other students without provocation. Once, with four adults present and in his immediate vicinity, he threw a thick plastic cafeteria bowl down on the table hard enough to smash it into bits, sending pieces exploding within close proximity of other students. Occupational and physical therapists, speech-lan-guage pathologists, and volunteers, served Patrick one-on-one most of each day, yet no one was able to predict or stop his outbursts, which escalated in frequency and duration.

Now Patrick could not be placed in time out in a playpen because he could climb out. How could we contain these wild, seemingly unprovoked tantrums which threatened the other students? Should we build a time out box for a three-year-old? Should we close him in a room, alone? How should we explain his plaintive wails to the preschoolers and the other students in the school who heard their sad echoes throughout the hallways?

We asked for help. We called a behavior management specialist from a nearby university to observe and give recommendations. He praised the consistency with which we were addressing Patrick's behavioral difficulties. At this time, since Patrick could not be contained in the playpen, the assistant or the teacher was physically removing him from the class when his outbursts were dangerous to himself or other children. He was held using an approved non-harmful physical restraint technique. The person who trained Patrick's management team commented that he had never known of the necessity to use such a restraint on a preschool-age student. When Patrick stopped the physical aggression, whoever was with him rocked him or walked him, talking soothingly to him until he was calm enough to return to the classroom. These physical restraint techniques became necessary more and more often, sometimes occupying the majority of Patrick's time in school.

The morale of the classroom teacher, her assistant, and the outside specialists serving the classroom was sinking quickly. Those who worked most closely with Patrick were showing signs of stress. Sometimes the teacher's voice sounded angry when she spoke to Patrick. Articles about the effects of substance abuse in utero were passed amongst all of us. Yes, Patrick did exhibit most of the characteristics described in the articles; this we could confirm. But what should we do? The few suggestions offered were all strategies that we had already tried in the classroom. One-on-one instruction, consistent responses, provision of a calm and nurturant environment, insurance of success—these were all in place.

We attended professional conferences focused on behavior management of children born to substance-abusing mothers. We attended with great hopes of hearing new suggestions, only to be disappointed when no new ideas were offered. Patrick was making no educational or social progress, and surely that of his classmates was being hindered. Margaret insisted that we were too soft on him and again offered us her permission to beat him. When she came to school and publicly beat him because she was tired of the teacher's notes, social services was notified and the decision was made not to invite her back into the classroom.

We hired an assistant for Patrick so that the programs of the other students could continue with less interruption. At this point, however, the tension was apparent in the entire classroom. His classmates may have been young and developmentally delayed, but they too were aware that at any moment there could be an outburst that would set everyone on edge, if not place them in danger of physical harm. We trained the teacher's assistant to react consistently to Patrick's inappropriate behaviors—to ignore those that could be safely ignored; redirect him from frustrating activities; restrain wild, aggressive behaviors; and provide loving, calm reassurance when the tantrums subsided. Because Patrick was spending increasingly longer times out of the classroom, we supplied the assistant with puzzles and activities that were appropriate to Patrick's ability and would not cause frustration. Food was always available, as Patrick's appetite in school appeared greatly out of proportion for his size. He often ate three bowls of cereal with milk and fruit as soon as he got off of the school bus and was hungry enough to eat another substantial meal an hour later. We kept social services abreast of the problems through frequent phone calls and letters documenting our concerns.

In February, Patrick was moved to another preschool class in the same building. This class had older students who were bigger and more able to defend themselves. We thought that Patrick might be less likely to strike out at larger, more verbal students. We encouraged him to use his words to discuss his anger or frustrations. A short "honeymoon" period quickly gave way to the same aggression inflicted upon these students. Bigger or not, no one wanted to take on Patrick, and the second class began to suffer from the tension of never knowing when toys would be flung across the room or someone would be kicked, bitten, or pinched.

On one visit to the second classroom, I sat and worked at a pegboard with Patrick. He had chosen this activity and was happily and ably placing pegs in the holes when, without explanation and quicker than I could react, he picked the entire wooden board off of the table and flung it like a discus across the room. Pure luck would have it that no little heads were in the path of this flying object. Patrick's response to my calm statement, "This was not what we do with the pegboard," was to begin to flail wildly at me with his little fists. I was the one to take him from the room and restrain him for 25 minutes as he screamed and head-butted me. All the while, I repeated, "You're a good boy, and I'll let you go as soon as you stop hitting" in the calmest voice I could muster, my heart pounding near to breaking, my mind racing as I fought back the tears for this tiny, fragile being so full of anger and pain. When he finally stopped fighting, the little body slowly slackening, I held him and rocked him until he nestled into me like an infant. Who had ever nurtured this little boy, I wondered? Who had ever held him and let him feel the love that all humans need to feel? And, looking to the future, who would ever love him enough to make this pain go away?

That school year ended with no problems solved. There were no solutions, only increasingly serious problems. The entire elementary school in which the preschool program was housed had been negatively affected by Patrick's loud and obvious presence, and two classes of preschoolers were visibly tense and frightened by this poor little boy. No help was forthcoming from his foster mother, and social services refused to respond to our pleas for consideration of the appropriateness of his placement with Margaret. I had learned that one of Margaret's teenaged sons had been identified as emotionally disturbed and that there was documentation that he had exposed himself to other boys in the school bathroom. Questions of possible sexual abuse were constantly in my mind, but this was confidential information and I could not use it against his foster family. All summer I considered what to do for this disturbed youngster.

Patrick was placed on the caseload of a preschool teacher who was the mother of three young boys. She was experienced in preschool and emotional disturbance and, although I hesitated to break the news of her most challenging student to her, when I told her she did not wince at serving him. Because she was the third preschool teacher in that elementary school, she was completely familiar with the problems that Patrick presented. The plan that we developed was that she would work with Patrick in his home for a short period in order to minimize his jealousy of other students' relationships with the teacher and to minimize his frustrations with learning tasks. He would begin to attend school gradually, and his time would be increased as he exhibited the ability to cope with classroom requirements. The second part of the plan called for a full evaluation by a local child development clinic, which we hoped would provide suggestions for successful integration of Patrick into the preschool program.

I met with Margaret in her home to introduce this plan. What I encountered on my first visit was a hostile woman who criticized the school system for being "too soft" with Patrick. While she yelled at me, Patrick stood in the corner of the neat, clean living room sucking his three fingers and rubbing his head. When I initiated conversation with Patrick, whom I had now known for almost two years, he only looked sheepishly at Margaret. "Say something to her!" she shouted at Patrick, which he did. I could extract no spontaneous conversation from him, nor would he come near me. Likewise, he did not enter Margaret's physical space, remaining far off in the corner, three fingers in mouth, hand rubbing head. The living room contained a white sofa and two white chairs (spotless), a glass coffee table, and other tables laden with small china knick-knacks. There were no toys in sight. The only other rooms in the house, which I did not enter, were the kitchen and bedrooms. I knew from past reports that Patrick shared Margaret's bedroom; she was a single parent. There were no children's toys in the yard.

In Patrick's presence, Margaret complained loudly that she might give him up because she didn't get enough money to keep him. I silently prayed that she would do just that. This very large (fat) woman also complained that this very frail little boy—below the fifth percentile for weight for his age—was eating her out of house and home. I tried to be direct and explained that his need for food was perhaps related to his need for nurturance, as he had been abandoned by his mother. I tried to explain how disturbed we felt his behavior to be and how deeply he seemed to need security. I tried, but I, like Patrick, was intimidated by this loud, mean woman who sat yelling back at all of the points that I tried to make. Without contradicting her, I let her lecture me as to how all of Patrick's problems stemmed from his first few months with his natural mother. I didn't tell her what I believed—that she was equally, if not more responsible than his natural mother for his disturbed behavior. I left grimly satisfied that I had gotten permission to implement the plan for home-based education, hopeful that a new strategy would make a difference. Margaret had also agreed to request a full evaluation for Patrick from the local child development agency and I, naively, hoped that help would be forthcoming from these experts.

My dual plan was a dual failure. The new teacher, Caitlin, was unable to establish any rapport with Patrick in his home due to Margaret's interference. He was compliant but non-interactive, sucking those three fingers and vigorously rubbing his head almost non-stop. Even when Margaret was out of sight, his glance stayed fearfully in the direction to which she had gone. She might go out of sight, but she was always within hearing range, ready to shout at either Patrick or Caitlin.

The report written by the local child development clinic documented that Patrick vacillated between two emotional/behavioral styles, at times being shy, quiet and withdrawn and at other times exhibiting aggressive, destructive, and demanding behavior. Although they noted that this behavior is typical of a young child who has been traumatized, they did not take on the larger issue of whether the trauma was in fact on-going. Margaret and Patrick were observed in a separation-reunion procedure conducted to examine Patrick's attachment to his mother. It was noted that Margaret made no attempt to include Patrick, nor did she encourage him in any of his own play. The interactions clearly reflected Patrick's submission to his foster mother's goals as he worked hard to please her and follow her lead. Their interactions did not afford Patrick the opportunity to gain experience with moderate, reciprocal, and supervised amounts of control over his behavior. Patrick would benefit from a gradual transfer of some power from Margaret to teach him to control his own behavior according to acceptable limits. His behavior revealed a strong need for adult attention, nurturance, and physical contact. He would benefit, the report concluded, from a great deal of physical affection, emotional support, and confidence-building praise and encouragement.

We knew what Patrick needed—had known this before the report was written. What were their recommendations regarding school? That we continue with our services and our plan for reintegration into the preschool class. That was all that they wrote! As we feared, the changes we wanted lay in Margaret's hands. Family and individual therapy were also recommended. She refused. I contacted social services. This time I wrote a pleading three-page letter to the director of the child protective services division begging for reconsideration of Patrick's placement with Margaret. I asked that they exert pressure on Margaret to take part in the recommended counselling. I wrote painstakingly, attempting to emphasize the extreme seriousness and uniqueness of this situation. Six weeks after I mailed the letter, a caseworker called to ask if I wanted to lodge a complaint! I was both outraged and outspoken. She said that she would investigate and get back to me. She never has.

I called the health department to report that Patrick seemed to be losing weight. The public health nurse who had originally referred him said that he had always been a "red flag case", but that Margaret had stopped bringing him in for scheduled physicals. I wondered how that happened with a "red flag case" but was satisfied with the knowledge that the nurse guaranteed me that she would send a van out to pick him up for his physical if Margaret was uncooperative. The van was used. The sight of Patrick's bony frame brought tears to her eyes, the public health nurse soon reported. He was to be hospitalized for failure to thrive. If non-medical causes of failure to thrive could be proven, there would be grounds for social services to remove Patrick from Margaret's home. Horribly, I prayed that Patrick would be found to be malnourished!

I am not certain of what was found in the hospital, as I was curtly informed by the hospital social worker that without a release from Margaret he could tell me nothing. Margaret refused to sign a release. Patrick is still skinny, Margaret is still fat, nothing has changed.

As his third year of preschool ends, Patrick attends only three days a week for an hour and a half each day. Margaret is often not home when the car brings Patrick home from his shortened day at school. Then he must be driven back to school and the teacher must spend time on the telephone tracking Margaret down. If Patrick's demeanor has changed in any way, it has become sadder and more withdrawn. On a recent visit to the classroom, I observed Patrick unexpectedly walk over to the slide and lay his little head down and sob. Defeat marked his shaking little form. His teacher held him gently and I left, tears rolling down my own cheeks for the boy that I don't know how to help.

Questions for Reflection

What are educators' legal and ethical duties in cases like Patrick's? Given what you know about this case and Candace's frustration, what would you suggest she do next? To what extent are the problems in this case matters of family or home environment? (Hallahan & Kauffman, Chapters 1, 2, and 4)

What aspects of this case illustrate multiple and severe disabilities? (Hallahan & Kauffman, Chapter 13)

To what extent might Margaret's attitudes and discipline of Patrick be explained by cultural factors? Could Margaret's approach to dealing with Patrick be justified as culturally acceptable and appropriate? (Hallahan & Kauffman, Chapter 3)

Early childhood special education is supposed to involve collaboration of families and all service agencies working with the child. Where did the problem lie in the failure of individuals and agencies to work together for Patrick's benefit? (Hallahan & Kauffman, Chapter 2)

Based on the information in this case, do you think Patrick's teachers were using appropriate behavior management procedures? Can you make any suggestions for improvement in their methods? (Hallahan & Kauffman, Chapters 7 and 8)

Do you think Patrick fit the definition of a child with a disability? If not, how would you define his problems? If so, what do you think were Patrick's most significant disabilities?

Praying for a Miracle

Margaret Darcy

Peter Park has muscular dystrophy (MD). His family lives in the city within a Korean community. His dad speaks English, but he struggles to communicate effectively. Peter's older sisters have been successful in school and are in college. Mr. Park can quote the scores his daughters obtained on entrance exams to highly competitive city high schools and laments the fact that they missed acceptance by a few points. His mother and grandmother assume a great deal of responsibility for Peter's physical care. Peter speaks Korean at home and arrived at school speaking no English.

At the age of three Peter entered our preschool program. We are a special school for children with physical disabilities and other health impairments. His previous teachers raved about him as a student and a person, but all expressed deep concern for his reticence and apparent sadness. One of the teachers told me that her personal goal that year had been to get him to smile.

Peter came to my classroom for fifth and sixth grade and is one of the brightest, most curious students I've taught in 25 years. On state exams in English language arts and math, Peter scored at the mastery level. On the *Key Math* exam, given twice a year in our school, Peter scored at the high school senior level while in sixth grade!

Peter's enthusiasm for learning is astonishing. I don't think it's just to please his parents. He wants to know everything! I would frequently slip in challenging vocabulary words during group discussions. Peter would immediately ask, "Mrs. Darcy, what does that mean?" Later I would hear him use the word or see it in his writing. After Peter outperformed his classmates in "Social Studies Jeopardy," his friend Mark exclaimed with a mix of envy and exasperation, "Are you a genius? How do you *do* that?" Peter calmly explained his method of study. The other kids were a bit disappointed that studying was the magic secret to Peter's success. It's obvious that his family is very supportive of good study habits and assists him in his work. Although there was a degree of jealousy among classmates who were not doing as well, Peter remained quite well liked for his droll sense of humor and his willingness to help others. Plus, he never bragged!

Pete's MD requires him to use a power wheelchair. He's really a good "driver" and tools around school with his best friend, Manuel, a Hispanic student who is Peter's equal in academics. Peter and Manuel earned the nickname "math maniacs" for their enthusiasm and accomplishments in that subject.

Peter enjoys the independence his power wheelchair gives him in school. Unfortunately, when he goes home he's transferred into a manual chair, which requires someone else to push him. His house is not wheelchair accessible, and Peter's dad carries him on his back up the stairs leading from the street to his home. Last year our physical and occupational therapy staff made home visits and assisted the family in obtaining the proper equipment for bathing and toileting Peter. Adaptations to make the home accessible are in the planning stages. When Peter is not in school he rarely leaves home except to go to church.

The Parks are devout Christians and are members of a Korean Church. Each morning, Peter's parents wake him at 5:30 a.m. to bathe. He then goes to church from 6:30–7:30 and gets home just in time to catch the bus to school. He does this every day. They are praying for a miracle. They are praying that Peter's MD will be cured. When a religious leader visits their church, Peter's dad picks him up from school to go to church and have this minister pray for Peter.

His morning schedule means that Peter does not have time for breakfast. A few months into the school year I realized that Peter did not eat anything at home in the morning. He never asked for breakfast, which some other children had in school. He finally agreed to eat with his classmates. I was happy about that because he had been awake for seven hours without food! When I mentioned to his father that breakfast was important, he said the family was worried about Peter's weight. He's getting bigger and heavier and his muscles are profoundly weak. Mr. Park felt that skipping breakfast would keep Peter from gaining weight. He also was adamant that Peter be given strenuous exercise to help make him stronger. He hoped that we would offer Peter wrestling and karate because he himself held an advanced belt in karate. He wants Peter to develop muscle tone. His repeated discussions with our school physician and physical therapists related to the real limits of the physical disability of MD seemed to fall on a closed mind.

During Peter's annual review, the psychologist (also Korean) from Peter's home school district spoke very movingly to Mr. Park about the emotional impact this inability to accept the disability was having on Peter. She was very sensitive to cultural issues and finally arranged for Peter to participate in a support program in his community where he received some individual counseling.

In school, Peter had a computer with an on-screen keyboard and/or a mini keyboard to facilitate writing. He often chose not to use them and instead wrote by hand, which was laborious for him. His handwriting was very tiny and faint due to his limited range of motion and general weakness. He would often stop and rest. During a parent conference, I asked his dad if there was a computer that Peter could use at home. He said it was downstairs and that he couldn't get Peter down there. I suggested that it be moved, but Mr. Park said there was no room. In our conversation, I brought this subject up again and showed Mr. Park a sample of Pete's handwritten work. I commented that it would take less time and be less tiring if it was done on a computer. Mr. Park seemed frustrated with me and said that if Peter would only press harder on the pen and pencil it would be okay. He said I needed to give him more practice every day in penmanship so his muscles would get stronger. As before, I tried to say that Peter tried very hard in everything he did but that these weaknesses were due to his disability and not because he wasn't trying. I did not convince him. He would repeat that Peter should try harder and that he does not know why he has this disability since no one else in the family ever had it.

This lack of acceptance on the part of his family has taken a toll on Peter. The staff was concerned for a while about his lack of affect and saw signs of depression. We provided counseling as part of his IEP, yet his dad opposed this and claimed that he was not depressed. Mr. Park said that that's just how Korean people are.

As Peter has gotten older, his relationships with his peers have become stronger. They provide a source of respect and acceptance. To our surprise, he received a Game Boy for Christmas, causing my assistant to moan that our model student was turning into an American boy. I admit to being happy to be able to scold Peter to put the game away after recess and get to work. He smiled.

Peter delivered the commencement address, along with his best friend Manuel, at elementary graduation. He wrote most of it himself, and it was beautiful. His mom was beaming and gave me flowers and a warm hug.

It's hard to know when to push a parent and how much to say. These are parents who love their child. They have demonstrated their appreciation of our efforts for their son. I know that Peter had a good experience academically, and I'm pretty sure that socially he made progress. But every day his family prays that he be "fixed." Every day Peter receives the message that he's not trying hard enough and that he is upsetting his parents.

I don't think I made a dent in Peter's father's attitude toward his son. At what point do we just accept a child where he is? Who am I to even ask that question? He's not *my* child, as much as I care for him. Our principal suggested to Peter's father that he look ahead a few years and seek a placement for high school in a mainstream program for gifted students. I share the concern of many staff members that at the time when MD can become most debilitating Peter will not have the support of professionals who understand the disability. He also won't have the support of his peer group of students who, like himself, have physical disabilities.

I think Peter is already a miracle of courage, determination, kindness, wit, intelligence, and perseverance.

Questions for Reflection:

What are the particular multicultural aspects of this case? Which, if either, do you think created greater problems for Peter—his family's Korean identity or his family's religion? (Hallahan & Kauffman, Chapter 3)

What were the advantages and disadvantages of Peter's attending a special school for students with physical disabilities? (Hallahan & Kauffman, Chapter 14)

Supposing that you were Mrs. Darcy, what, if anything, would you have attempted that she did not in trying to address Peter's education, disability, culture, or family?

Supposing that you were receiving teacher of Peter in a high school program in a regular school, what would be your primary concerns? (Hallahan & Kauffman, Chapter 14)

Filling Mr. K's Shoes—Not!!

Susan Washko

"What else can I try?" The words repeated themselves in my head in time to my feet hitting the sidewalk. This evening walk through my neighborhood was supposed to be a stress reliever, but today it was just extended pacing.

Following a year as a full-time student completing my master's degree, I'd taken a job on a one-year contract, filling in for a teacher on educational sabbatical. I was responsible for teaching sixth- through eighth-grade students in high-level academic language arts/reading classes. The curriculum in each grade consisted of multi-disciplinary units based on selected literature. I liked the idea of the curriculum. I knew it would be a challenge, because all three grades contained many materials I hadn't read or used. I thought I would enjoy the age level and energy of the kids, although my student teaching experience had been with high school students.

By mid-October I felt that I'd accomplished a fair amount in getting to know my students. With three preparations, I wasn't being as creative with the curriculum as I would've liked; I was often just one jump ahead of my students in reading, and scrambling for interesting activities. I provided enrichment activities when I could, and it seemed that I filled every spare waking moment with paperwork. The sixth- and seventh-graders were cooperative and worked well, and I was comfortable enough to relax and have fun with them at times. But that eighth-grade class . . .

The eighth-graders were a very bright, achievement-oriented group, accustomed to being assigned 25–35 pages of reading per day and, for the most part, doing it—along with vocabulary and long-range project work—as nightly homework for just this one class. Besides other classes' work, they had a variety of other interests to keep up with. Clay, easily the brightest student, already had a specialty. He devoured at least one book each week on the U.S. Civil War. He also had an interest in reading classic literature, as did Kevin, Shantelle, and Susan. Four or five of the other girls read adult-level romance novels non-stop. Bill didn't enjoy independent reading much, but he had followed a number of stocks since the sixth grade. There was a group of boys who lived for free time to spend on their personal computers and computer bulletin boards. Two other boys were gifted cartoonists and were developing portfolios of their work.

Allison had read every fan magazine article ever written on Guns N' Roses, I think. The other dozen's interests were far-flung. Many took instrument lessons, dance, or karate; many played sports. They had all had my predecessor for the last two years of language arts/reading classes, and many had clearly been jolted when "their" teacher announced that he was taking a sabbatical during their final middle school year.

From the first few days of the year, a number of the eighth graders had let it be known that they resented my presence. How dare I think I could lead a class in place of their beloved Mr. K? I'd been in a class with David, their teacher, in my master's program, and I readily understood their devotion. He's bright, witty, creative, a technology whiz, a writer of songs and poetry, and has the energy of any three normal people. He'd helped the enrichment program at the school evolve and had taught in this position for five years—lived in the community for many more years than that and had quite a following. I'm rather in awe of him myself.

The sixth and seventh graders had made the transition to being "my kids" pretty smoothly, I mused. They were, in the main, enjoying the class structure and curriculum. They participated enthusiastically in whole-class and small-group reading, writing, and discussion. We'd done some skits and projects, played some games, and so on. With these kids, I had few discipline problems. With all three grade levels, I'd spent time in "getting to know you" activities. Students made classroom rules in conjunction with me. I'd written students and parents letters, enclosing a syllabus and notes on my expectations.

My student teaching assignment had been with high, average, and remedial level tenth-and twelfth-grade classes in a different district, so this year was an adjustment, but I was fairly comfortable that I had made a solid beginning. I wanted to give students opportunities to direct more of their learning around the various themes, and I felt ready to do that with the eager and hard-working lower grades. With the eighth graders, I was more reluctant to take that risk, as so far they had given me little but resistance. Was it the assignments? The particular mix of students in that class? Me?

I spent a lot of time trying to understand how the eighth graders were feeling. They'd been very successful with David and had really enjoyed him. They'd established their comfort zone, had been ready to coast through this year familiar with his expectations and procedures. They felt deserted, and their first impulse, instead of trying new ways of doing things, was to complain and compare. How was I to deal with all of that? Expect tons of questions and challenges and explain patiently, I decided. Work hard to get them on my side. Be fair. And maybe hope for a little luck?

I had introduced the first unit, "Real People," and announced project options (from material left by David) including visual autobiography, audio or video recording of biographies, and research on local historical figures using courthouse and historical society documents. To Justin's sullen, "Why do we have to do this?" I'd explained the unit's place in the year-long thinking skills curriculum strand—that was clear from the curriculum guide. But the assignment and option were greeted by "WHY do we have to do this?" from a variety of questioners. I was less sure about the why of the day-to-day assignments myself—and I guess my lack of confidence showed. I found myself trying to avoid getting into confrontations over questions clearly designed to get under my skin. I became more careful about each assignment's purpose, so that I'd be able to meet students' questions. Soon, I was tying each assignment to others in the unit during my opening minute's overview of the day's activities; then I began calling on students to make those connections. That ended the questions, but new comments began: "That's stupid!" or "BOOOriiinnng!" or "Why do you have to ask us questions about what we read; why can't we just read?" In response I pulled out all of my goals for the unit and listed them. (Thank goodness for the curriculum guide!) Foot-dragging and grumbling continued. I referred to my experiences as a high school student and in student teaching to show how these skills fit into preparation for grades to come; still there was almost daily resistance to reading and writing assignments and discussions. I didn't know what to do with this question: "When are we going to do something fun?" So I counted it a draw when I at least kept back a sharp reply.

I wondered whether perhaps some of the assignments were too difficult or my expectations too high, so for a week I consciously chose easier readings and other work. That had no effect on the eighth graders' attitudes. They remained rebellious and dour.

Expectations and grades were clearly an ongoing issue—not only for these students, but for their parents as well. To allay their concerns, I'd double-checked to ensure that students knew the "look-for's" on each assignment and project. They'd done self-assessments periodically, as well. I was surprised when the first group of eighth- grade projects, whose grades were about two-thirds As, produced requests for four conferences—all of them parents inquiring about project grades in the B range. In fact, both of Bill's parents arrived at a conference to express their concern and disappointment; they said this was the first B he had ever received. That really shook me up! Were my assignments or grading really out of line? Other eighth graders' parents called to question the use of writing groups, the directions for assignments, some quiz questions. Although I was uncomfortable with what I thought was some parents' pushiness, I tried to remain calm and professional, just explaining and not getting defensive. With each call, my confidence suffered. When I was caught in an error, I apologized and made amends. The grades for the eighth-grade students were generally good, so I reasoned that the assignments must be mostly at an appropriate level. I'd thrown out a quiz that most of them bombed. They—and their parents—

probably just needed a little more time to get used to me. And maybe there were other things I could try to help their adjustment. But what?

Thinking that my other classes frequently enjoyed working in groups, I next considered using that option more often with the eighth graders. It seemed to me that group-structured lessons and projects might provide support and reassurance. Perhaps some of the eighth graders' resistance was motivated by worries about grades? But would groups just give them support for rebelling more against my lessons? I hoped not, and after several more frustrating days decided to give groups a try for a week. The students were somewhat more receptive to working, it appeared, when they could be with their friends. But it didn't take long for self-selected groups to raise a different concern; cliques became prominent. Bill, Dee, James, and Leigh (clearly the "in" group) accomplished their work quickly and were articulate in sharing with the class. But their rudeness when other groups led discussions or made presentations included snide remarks and outright laughter. I put a stop to the audible things quickly; they resorted to eye-rolling and suppressed giggling. Meanwhile, Becky, Anne, and Shantelle presented inaudibly; Jake, Sam, Mary, and Chrissy uniformly played for laughs; Aaron, Adam, and Jamie affected boredom no matter what; and Josh was always the last to find a group that would have him. Despite the challenges of the work and admonitions to stay on task until they completed the day's assignment, in any unwatched moments Allison, Stephanie, and Susan murmured about other students' clothes and hair, while Clay, Steve, and Kevin caught each other up on their latest computer exploits. The others were less predictable, but overall these groups didn't create an atmosphere I wanted to encourage, even though more work was being accomplished with less resistance. Would my choosing the groups help?

I asked a colleague who taught eighth-grade geography and who used groups about how often she assigned them versus how often she let the kids choose. Reassured by her response, that she chose the groups the majority of the time, I mapped out my choices. Before beginning to assign groups, I decided to address the class about my feeling on this issue. I explained the instructional reasons for group-structured lessons that I expected they'd enjoy. Without pointing fingers, I cited some of the undesirable results that I was seeing consistently and my battling with them about the groups they were choosing. A few of them had the grace to hang their heads, but the rest clamored their discontent.

James made a direct challenge. "Mr. K. never assigned groups!"

"There won't be any good groups," Zack chimed in, "if you assign them!"

Justin's "What does she do that's good?" stung, but I ignored it.

Taking a deep breath, I stuck by my decision. I allowed that perhaps our definitions of "good groups" were different, and said that since I'd already reminded them numerous times of my expectations about group work, this would be the way it'd be for a while. They left grumbling again. Now what? Even if students in the groups I assigned could work together, would they?

The tenor of the class concerned me and was wearing me down. The eighth graders had become a constant negative in my day. I was convinced that most of the assignment options for them were good ones, answering my goals and the curriculum's. Really concentrating on being familiar with the eighth-grade materials, I was somewhat neglecting the sixth and seventh graders' progress—and I resented that. I knew the eighth graders had worked on assignments this hard or harder for David. I had his handouts, folders, and notes. I'd certainly tried a number of presentation techniques and instructional strategies. Concerns about grading had been addressed. Still, every day brought continued conflict. The only way to change the eighth-grade class atmosphere was to get them allied with me about their learning. How was I to do that? What hadn't I tried? It was clearly unpopular and uncool to enjoy my class, or to do much of anything in there willingly. How could I turn that around?

Questions for Reflection

Susan seemed puzzled about the fact that she got along well with the sixth and seventh graders but had great difficulty with the eighth graders. How do you evaluate her thinking about why she is having this difficulty? What, if anything, do you think she is missing in her self-appraisal?

What particular instructional strategies do you think might have worked better with these eighth graders? (Hallahan & Kauffman, Chapter 15)

Some might suggest that Susan was trying too hard to be liked by her students and that she should have taken a more assertive and authoritarian stance with them. What might have been the advantages and disadvantages of taking such a stance with these students?

How do you think Susan measures up as a teacher of high-achieving or gifted students? That is, in what way(s) does she reflect what you believe are the ideal characteristics of a teacher of gifted students, and in what way(s) does she fall short? (Hallahan & Kauffman, Chapter 15)

Given that David is still in the area, what do you think Susan might have asked of him that might have helped her deal with her eighth grade students?

Never Give Up

Steven Browning

Over the summer, Emma Porter found out she had cancer. That September, she would have embarked on her 25th year of teaching. However, because of her diagnosis, Emma would be forced to stay home, undergo treatment, and, she hoped, regain her strength. Within weeks, she informed the principal of Parks Elementary, and they agreed that Emma would attempt a return to teaching in March. In the meantime, a long-term substitute had to be found.

Concerns about beginning the year with a substitute prompted the principal to call upon Michael Lawson, a veteran fifth-grade teacher who had recently retired. Michael agreed to begin the year but said he could only commit to a month or two. Two weeks later, he found himself standing before a classroom of 26 gifted and talented (GT) fifth graders.

"Good morning," began Michael, "and welcome to the first day of fifth grade. My name is Mr. Lawson and I will be your teacher for the next few weeks. As you probably already know from the letter that was sent home, Mrs. Porter, your assigned teacher, is out sick. In a month or two, you will have another teacher, a substitute, who will be here until Mrs. Porter's return."

Ryan Warner sat at a desk near the back wall of the classroom half-listening to Mr. Lawson's explanation. He was completely unaware of the situation but was not particularly interested. If a letter had been sent home, it would not have been unusual for Ryan's father to neglect to share its contents with him. As a single father of two and the manager of a large software company, David Warner did not have time to keep up with the details of school. That was his wife's specialty until she passed away; her death was a devastating blow to the family, but even more so for Ryan, because he was only in first grade when it happened. After his mother's death, Ryan received counseling to deal with anger issues that had surfaced but, after six months, David decided to end his son's counseling hoping, instead, that time would heal remaining wounds. Ryan had always done well in school, and now that he was 11, and in fifth grade, David hoped his son would assume more responsibility for his schooling and require fewer reminders to get homework done and study for tests. This would be particularly helpful to David, as his job required a fair amount of travel. Sometimes, he was out of the country for up to two weeks at a time. During those travel periods, David's mother looked after her son's children. Ryan's sister, Melissa, now a 16-year-old junior, was consumed with typical teenage concerns (e.g., friends, dating, parties, high school football games); she had no interest in following her brother's studies.

"Ryan," Mr. Lawson called again, "please move to your assigned seat."

Ryan was so intent on following the bird outside the window that he did not realize Mr. Lawson had called his name three times. On the fourth attempt, Ryan finally heard his name and moved to his new seat. Mr. Lawson had arranged the students in alphabetical order. Despite having to move, Ryan remained in the back; with this, he was pleased.

Soon, days turned into weeks, and the school year was underway. Mr. Lawson was following the curriculum and documenting students' progress and behavior in an effort to prepare things for the substitute, who would take over the class in mid-October. The school year, up to that point, had been relatively uneventful. Ryan had been involved in a few incidents with administrators (e.g., refusing to follow directions) and other students (e.g., arguing), but Mr. Lawson did not think there was cause for alarm. In his class of GT students, Charlie Moore and Abby Tucker were the only two receiving special education services. Charlie was receiving special services for his emotional disorder and, Abby, for her learning disability. Mr. Lawson was fascinated by the fact that giftedness could occur in combination with a learning disability.

At the beginning of October, Steven Browning found out that he would be inheriting Mrs. Porter's class until her return. At age 25, he had already been substituting for several years and had become so well known at Parks Elementary that he spent almost all of his substituting days there. Most recently, he had taken on a long-term substitute position in fourth grade that ended with the previous school year. He enjoyed substituting at Parks, but with a Bachelor of Arts degree in psychology he was happy to have begun coursework that would lead to certification as an elementary teacher. The administrators at Parks Elementary were eager to have him join their faculty. In fact, they said they would have a teaching position waiting for him as soon as he completed all the requirements for provisional certification.

It was clear that Steven would be one of those teachers students remembered long after their year-end farewells. He prided himself on making every effort to have a positive effect on every student with whom he came in contact. With every teaching assignment, he established a rapport with each of his students by treating them with respect and showing genuine interest in them as people. In addition, he modeled appropriate behavior and communicated high expectations. In his lessons, he conveyed clear objectives, gave explicit directions, used effective instructional strategies, asked questions, praised appropriate behavior, monitored students' understanding, and explained the importance of material. He believed that respect, genuine interest, high expectations, effective instruction, and assistance went a long way in instilling a desire to succeed within students.

In early October, Steven met with Michael Lawson to discuss the transition. Michael explained where he was in the curriculum and gave Steven advice on how to proceed. They discussed the students with whom Steven would be working and Michael tried to give him fair warning about potential problems.

"Jasmine Gray's mother calls a lot," he told Steven, "so be prepared to discuss her progress and give suggestions with respect to enrichment activities. Charlie Moore receives special education services for an emotional disorder, and Abby Tucker receives services because she has a learning disability. You should read their IEPs [Individualized Education Programs] to find out more about their disabilities; also, their goals and objectives are in there. You'll want to stay in close contact with the special education teacher. You might want to read the information in their cumulative folders for some background information. Ryan Warner is not receiving special services, but he has had a few behavior problems, so you'll want to keep an eye on him; his mother died when he was in first grade. I've spoken with his father a few times."

Steven spent several afternoons over the next two weeks preparing for his assignment. He reviewed the curriculum, spoke with the teachers on the fifth-grade team, and read IEPs and cumulative folders, as Michael had suggested. He also looked back at Michael's first-quarter progress reports, which had been sent home to parents. On Ryan Warner's progress report, Mr. Lawson had written:

> *Appears fully capable, but he is turning in incomplete work. I like him a great deal, but what comes out as cynicism or arrogance hurts his relationships.*

By mid-October, Steven was ready to take over the class. The transition, for the most part, was smooth. Parents had remained well informed, and many students were happy to see Steven, as they recognized him from previous substitute assignments. Within days, however, Steven took note of some aberrant behavior. One day, during a game of silent speedball, Ryan took the big, red rubber ball they were using for the game and threw it—with unusually high velocity—toward Sarah, one of his classmates. The ball hit her head, and Steven asked Ryan to sit out for the remainder of the game. Later, in his discussion with Ryan, Steven found out that Ryan had every intention of hitting Sarah with the ball; however, the reason for his deliberate act was unclear. In subsequent incidents, Steven noticed Ryan giving classmates unusually dirty looks or refusing to participate in activities. He also noticed that Ryan and Charlie had become close friends. Steven began to document Ryan's behavior and discussed the incidents with Ryan's father during their end-of-the-first-quarter conference. They agreed to continue to monitor Ryan's behavior and remain in close contact.

Steven Browning and his students continued through the month of November. One afternoon in early December, as Steven sat at his desk planning for the days and weeks ahead, the assistant principal stormed into his classroom.

"I had a terrible run-in with Ryan at lunch today. I caught him throwing food, asked him to stop, and he gave me a look unlike any I have ever seen. His attitude is disgusting . . . one of the worst in the school. I will see to it that he misses P.E. and recess tomorrow."

Steven listened intently as the assistant principal explained the incident. Then, he did his best to explain Ryan's situation without making excuses for him.

"Ryan's mother died when he was in first grade," Steven explained. "His father travels a lot on business; sometimes, when he's away, Ryan comes to school wearing the same shirt all week. His grandmother is supposed to be taking care of him when his father is on business, but I don't think Ryan gets along with her. I wonder, too, if the holidays are particularly hard for him."

With that explanation, the assistant principal softened a bit, but they agreed that Ryan needed some help.

The next day, Ryan had another run-in with the assistant principal. He was caught pushing another student in the lunch line, and when the assistant principal asked Ryan to follow her to the office, Ryan refused. With teeth and fists clenched, he said, "Don't tell me what to do! I'm already missing P.E. and recess. Are you gonna tell me I can't eat lunch?"

That afternoon, Steven spoke with Ryan about the incidents in the cafeteria. Ryan, who seemed well aware and mature, often acknowledged his wrongdoing, admitted his behavior was inappropriate, but provided no explanation for it. Sometimes, he'd simply say, "I'm rebelling." After school, Steven called Ryan's father to discuss the incidents and set up a conference for the following week. Mr. Warner agreed.

During the conference, which took place just before the winter break, Steven went over much of the same information he had already discussed over the phone with Ryan's father.

"Ryan seems most likely to misbehave when he is not in the classroom, like during lunch, recess, specials. He and I have discussed the fact that, when he becomes angry, upset, or uncomfortable, a certain negative attitude emerges. Other students, teachers, and administrators, then, react to that negative attitude and an unpleasant incident usually follows. I have suggested alternative ways of dealing with those feelings, like remaining calm and speaking respectfully. Some days, he does very well. As I mentioned to you on the phone, I think we should try a behavior contract. Also, you might want to consider outside counseling for Ryan. As you know, our school counselor has been working with him, but she has to work with a lot of students. Ryan seems to need more than what she can give him."

Mr. Warner seemed receptive to Steven's suggestions, and they proceeded to work out the details of the contract. They had only to figure out what rewards Ryan could earn each week; for that, they invited Ryan into the conference.

After a detailed explanation, it was apparent that Ryan understood his responsibilities with respect to the contract. They settled on rewards, and Steven asked each conference participant to sign.

For three weeks after the winter break, the contract seemed to be working well. Then, without warning, Ryan seemed to revert back to his old ways. In science, he refused to work with his partner and nearly brought him to tears with the comments he made. Later, he purposely walked into another student. Steven called home. Mr. Warner had always seemed receptive to Steven's comments and observations, but, this time his support seemed to be waning.

"Ryan told me about the incident in science today," explained Mr. Warner, "and he told me that it was *his* partner who refused to work with *him*, not the other way around. I don't know what to think about all this."

Steven was disheartened by Mr. Warner's reaction. Was he, now, denying his son's behavior issues? Why?

Behavior Contract

I, Ryan Warner, agree to:

- continue to act appropriately in class and
- act appropriately outside of class (during lunch, recess, P.E., music, art, assemblies, library, etc.).

I understand that acting appropriately means I will:

- listen to and follow directions,
- speak respectfully and positively with everyone (students, teachers, lunch staff, etc.), and
- remain calm when upset and/or angry.

Each day, I can earn up to one point:

- 1 point   =   appropriate behavior all day
- .5 point   =   appropriate behavior most of the day
- 0 points   =   inappropriate behavior part of or all day

A possible 5 points can be earned by the end of each week:

- 5 points   =   paperback book
- 4.5 points   =   video game rental
- 4 points   =   move
- 3.5 points   =   movie rental
- 3 points   =   ice cream

Signatures:

_____
Ryan Warner (student)   Date

_____
Mr. Warner (father)   Date

_____
Mr. Browning (teacher)   Date

_____
Mrs. Ford (counselor)   Date

Questions for Reflection

Did Ryan have a disability, or was he a gifted student whose behavior was somewhat problematic, but not a disability? (Hallahan & Kauffman, Chapters 5, 7, 8, and 15)

If Ryan had a disability, what was it? And if he had a disability, what should be done about it?

Given that two of the students in this class of gifted students (Charlie and Abby) had been identified as having disabilities (emotional and learning disabilities, respectively), what kind of accommodations do you think their teacher should have made for them? (Hallahan & Kauffman, Chapters 6, 8, and 15)

What are the best features and the relative weaknesses of the behavioral contract as it is written?

How should Mr. Browning respond to Mr. Warner's description of what Ryan told him? (Hallahan & Kauffman, Chapter 4)

How and to what extent do you think Ryan's life experiences might have affected the way he behaved in school? How should life experiences be taken into consideration in determining whether a student has a disability and in devising a behavior management strategy? (Hallahan & Kauffman, Chapters 3, 4, and 8)